DESCRIBING LIFE: MONOLOGS FOR WOMEN

Jolene Goldenthal

Copyright 2007 by Jolene Goldenthal

Published by Bleich Books

BleichBooks@yahoo.com

Second printing 2009.

ISBN: 978-0-9789087-0-6

Cover art: Carol Goldenthal

Printed in U.S.A
Morris Publishing

We redeem our mothers' lives
In ways we never knew
In ways we never dreamt...

Thanks to the Editors of these publications who first published:
A FLOWER OR SOMETHING, in *Best Women's Stage Monologues*, (Smith and Kraus) A FLOWER OR SOMETHING in *Millennium Monologues,* (Meriwether) THE ONE, in *Best Women's Stage Monologues*, (Smith and Kraus) a segment of BIRTHDAY in *Monologues For Women By Women* (Heinemann), and WIFE TO TOLSTOI in *Mequasset By The Sea & Other Plays* (Andrew Mt. Press).

Other Plays by Jolene Goldenthal

HOW WE MET AND OTHER EVENTS
MYRA AND...
THE OTHER SONYA
REMEMBERING RACHEL
MEQUASSET BY THE SEA
THE STATION PLAYS:
     MIGRATION
     LEFTY ON A BENCH
     GEORGIE, GOODBYE
     BUDDIES
     ZIG – ZAG
THE RETRO BUS
TOM'S HUSBAND (adapt. Sarah Orne Jewett)
TAPESTRY
FATHER'S DAY
THE BEAUTIFUL TRUTH
HOW TO EAT A PIZZA
ISLAND
THE CARRIAGE
I THOUGHT I SAW A SNOWMAN
MRS CROWLEY AND THE SOCIAL WELFARE
A STRANGER IN A STRANGE LAND
THE YELLOW LEAF

INTRODUCTION

Monolog is an ancient form of performance. Here is the actor, alone on the stage, telling tales, confiding secrets, sharing laughter or tears with the audience...

One actor does it all. She can become whoever she chooses, hiding her thoughts and feelings from the audience, fooling them into believing her tears, her laughter, perhaps her lies as well.

These fifty original monologs were created to give the actor multiple ways to conceal or reveal herself. I've aimed to provide a range of age-appropriate pieces suited for audition, for performance, for class work or for study.

Several of the monologs in this collection have won awards. Others are so new that you may be the very first to work on them.

A monolog is an opportunity.
The actor makes it happen.
Break a leg!

Jolene Goldenthal

DESCRIBING LIFE

CONTENTS:

CONTENTS:

Mattie enters, waving one hand very very carefully in the air.

A FLOWER OR SOMETHING

I've got something everybody wants. I'm not kidding. You look at me and you go 'What?' Which only shows you don't know beans. (She waggles her fingers in an exaggerated gesture).

There's nobody's got what I've got. Honest. I'm going into the book. I was just like anybody else. Honest. Then it happened. I got dumped. This guy I thought was so great. Answer to my prayers and all. Well, okay. I've been dumped before. But this time I get dumped one night and the next morning, the very next morning...Are you ready for this? The very next morning I get fired. (pause)

Well. That was a bit much. I sat down and I thought that what I need is something to make me different. Like outstanding. No guy is going to dump me like I am Ms. Nobody. And no boss is going to fire me if I don't want to be fired. (raising her hand)

So I think, 'What?' Miss America I'm not. So that's out. I figure maybe shave my head. But I don't know. I'm kind of attached to my hair. Get a motorcycle? Zoom around? Mucho bucks. Let that go. I keep on thinking and then it comes to me. Nails.

Really long nails. Everybody wants them. It's a business, f'Chris-sake. Those dinky little plastic fakes. Paste them on, ruins your nails underneath. So that's when it came to me. Really long nails. All I had to do was wait. No cost. Nothing.

So I think like one hand. Let them grow on one hand, keep the other hand short. So I do it. And they grow like crazy. So by now I'm getting some attention. I've got people, strangers, asking me, 'How're the nails today?' And I begin to worry, you know. I mean, I've been lucky. But still...maybe I'm supposed to put some kind of cream on them or something. Maybe eat

1

something special. Forget it. They grow. They grow so one of them curls itself around another one and I tell you, it is some sight.

At night sometimes when I'm not doing anything, say maybe it's a tummy going ouch on the tube, or one of those headache things, I stretch out my hand. I hold it near the light and it looks like something. A flower or something. Or curly fries, maybe. I figure I'm ready for the book. Okay. A couple more inches maybe, and I'm really ready.

Somebody told me about some Chinese emperors way back. They let their nails grow really long to show they never had to work, or something. But, hey, I'm working every day. Oh, yeah. I got a new job. No problem. (she laughs)

There's this guy comes in where I work. He sits around, watching me. So this one day he's sitting and watching and he goes, "What're y' tryin' for? Disability? Y' wanna be disabled? Sit home an' collect?"

I take a deep breath. I smile. He's a customer, after all. "It's only the one hand," I tell him nicely, like I don't give a care.

So this character goes, "It's a hand. Not a fuckin' ornament!"

He shakes his head, sort of sad. "So what's it all about?" he goes, "What goes on upstairs?"

Well. I feel like giving him a good slap in the face or something. But then I figure he's not worth it. Here I'm maybe ready for the book and I had my picture in the paper...

I think like this. What's Madonna got? Nerve. And Julia? That big smile. And me? I've got my nails. (She holds up her hand, admiring, and slowly, very slowly, she exits.)

2

She walks slowly, carefully, across the stage, holding a small stuffed dog. She places the dog on a chair, arranging it with care. She studies it, turns away, and walks back, talking to the dog as she goes.

THE DOG'S SPANISH LESSON

So. (pause) Okay. (pause) You gonna help me out here? You gonna help me out or you just gonna sit there...like...like a dog? (to the dog) I'm counting on you. I'm counting on you to help me figure out what I'm gonna do...if he shows up...Okay? (she turns now to talk to an unseen someone, turning away from the dog).

So. Hi there...Pop. What's the good word Pop? (pause) So. You're back. You're back, huh? (pause) For how long, Pop? Long time no see. How've you been...and all? Had a good trip...wherever? (pause) Yeah. Mom's okay. She manages. She always sort of...manages. (pause) Those times you walked out...she managed. Yeah. (long pause) That last time...When was that now? (pause) I was just a kid. Supper time. We ate early. Hot dogs and beans. (pause) Yeah. Sure I remember. I have this weird habit. I remember things...things like that...(she gestures to her head) They *stick here*...right here. (pause)

It was maybe six o'clock. Still light out. You get up from the table. Kind of stretch and pat your tummy. You gave a sort of wave at us...Mom and me...and then you go, 'Adios amigos! Time for the dog's Spanish lesson' and wham-slam out the door. You thought it was funny. Well I'm here to tell you...NOT. NOT FUNNY. (pause)

3

I hopped up from the table and ran quick to the door. I guess I figured I'd go with you...if I was quick enough. But you were one swift mover, Pop. One, two – out the door!

So which way did you go, huh? I could never figure it out. (pause) Mom...she'd kind of smile and start to clear away the dishes. 'Let him go, baby,' she'd say, 'Let him go. He always comes back.'

BUT YOU DIDN'T! YOU DIDN'T COME BACK! YOU NEVER CAME BACK! (a long pause) So okay, Pop. YOU CAN'T GO! YOU CAN'T GO ANYWHERE! (She turns desperately, running to pick up the dog) THE DOG'S HERE, POP! I'VE GOT THE DOG!

(She turns, clutching the dog to her, looking off...waiting.)

Tessa's mom meets a challenge.

TESSA'S MOM

I'm here to get my tummy stitched. (pause) Yeah. (pause) See...uh...I know you're never going to believe this...But...see...I used to be three hundred pounds. (pause) Yeah. (pause) Honest. All my life practically. Yeah. Three hundred pounds. In my family...in my family...there was nobody...Nobody like me. Nobody could figure it out. Why me? It got them going, y'know. They were after me all a' the time. (pause) Yeah. (a small laugh)

My brother in law...my sister's husband...he even said he'd give me a hundred dollars...one hundred dollars...if I could only stop eating...(pause) Yeah...One hundred dollars to stop eating. And that's pretty good money, y'know. He said like this. "Look," he said. "One hundred dollars on the button the day you do some serious not eating." Well I tried, y' know. I really did try. Cut out doughnuts. Cut out ice cream...and boy...those are...I guess I should say were...my favorites. It didn't do any good. I guess giving them up for a week wasn't enough...

So anyhow, what happened is my little girl. I have a little girl...Tessa...Five years old. Going on six. (pause) She is just the sweetest little thing. Tiny. (a gesture) About so high. (pause) She's going to school now. Kindergarten. Oh boy. So there she is in that old kindergarten...Little tables and chairs just so big...

I'm kind of embarrassed to tell you this...But here goes (pause) I went over to the kindergarten one day and the teacher said, 'Hi. You're Tessa's mom. Have a seat.'

Well, I went to sit down and you know what happened...I couldn't. I couldn't squeeze myself in any of those little chairs. (pause) I went home and I said to myself, 'This is it. This is it for sure.' There's my Tessa over in that school with all those tiny chairs...And here's her mother – can't even get herself to sit in

5

one of them. What am I supposed to do? Wait until she gets to the high school and then maybe I can squeeze myself into a seat and talk to a teacher?

And that was the day I did it. I made up my mind and I did it. My brother in law said it was too damn bad I waited so long. But he kept his word. Oh, yeah, he did, and I bought new clothes with the money. Had to. After a while everything I owned looked like rags on me. Oh, yeah. But now there's this tummy business. You don't think about it when you're so busy tossing out all the goodies from the breadbox. I even tossed all a' my cookbooks. They made me hungry just looking at them, f'Pete's sake!

So now there's this operation. My tummy. (a sigh) It's just nothing. I'm gonna have myself cut and stitched...And boy will I look great when I walk into that school and the teacher says, 'Take a seat' and I do! Yeah.

(she smiles proudly and walks out)

Susie comes home.

SURVIVING

I tried to get myself on one of those shows. Those survivor things. I mean...you know...big bucks if I could...like...survive.

I seriously thought about the show where they sling you over a kind of a mountain with maybe some really deep dark water waiting for you underneath when you fall out...(pause). But I don't know...

I heard about one where they pay you to move into a tiny apartment with a whole bunch of people you never even saw before...And they keep a camera on you the whole time. Whoops! Pass on that.

I tried to get myself on a show where you think you are a hot designer if you could only...you know...like design. (pause) Didn't make the cut.

Then there is this cooking show. (pause) You get to wear a great hat! To be honest, I really don't cook...I mean...you know...eat yeah...cook...no. So I had to forget about that...(pause).

But then I get a break. I get myself in line for a job working for the Big Man. Well...I had to look good. So I figured I'd lose about twenty pounds. Twenty pounds missing from me and I would look *so terrific*! So I quit eating for about a month and I've got to tell you I looked *terrific*! (she turns slowly, elegantly, terrific)

I fly to New York. I am *so excited*. I get to see the Big Man...Well...His secretary/assistant...whatever. She starts out asking me a whole lot of questions...and guess what? I pass out. Yeah. Right there. Right there in her office. I never even get to see the Big Man. (pause). But I've got to tell you...*I looked terrific!* (sigh).

7

So now I'm in line for a restaurant job. Yeah. I figure I've got a really good crack at it, the way I really like to eat and everything. And nobody probably even cares if I am maybe a tiny bit...not thin. But it is really hard work and you have to beat out a whole lot of other people who probably tried out for the cooking show...and the designer show...and maybe the really deep water show...

So I don't know...(pause) I'm thinking maybe...maybe go home. Find a job. A plain old boring job where maybe I get to sit down a whole lot. Or maybe...maybe...start a little business...doing...something...(to the audience) Got any ideas? Maybe we can work out...something? What do you think? Call me, okay? (hopeful) I'm ready. I'm here. I'm in the book...

Marcie has a crisis in her car.

IT'S THE LAW BABY

So all right. What in the name of...? What am I supposed to do here? Turn off my phone while I'm driving through this rinky dink town? Because if I don't the cops'll get me? Yeah. Right.

Look. This phone is like my arm. Like my hand. Like my...my whatever! And I'm supposed to turn it off because some idiot decides to pass a stupid law? Well wow.

I am not going to do it. That's all there is to it. (pause) I can't do it. That's it.

I'll tell them. They stop me, I'll tell them. Hey, it's my right. I've got a right...I think...You're going to toss me in jail for talking on the phone? In my car? My very own car that I love so much? My sweet car that loves me back? You can just bet you...Yes, I'm mad! Sure I'm mad!

You're infringing on my what d'ya call it...MY RIGHTS! You're stepping on my rights! Isn't this supposed to be a free country? Or something?

Look. I pay my taxes. I vote. (pause) Well, yeah. That was a real screw-up. But I voted! I didn't vote for you buster, or your really stupid law...a law about a phone! But I voted. Yes, I did. And what good did it do me?

So now what? Now you're telling me I can't drive and talk at the same time? Well you listen here to me.

Listen good! You have kids? You run a business? You check up on your mother? (pause) Well sure. Sure I call her. 'Hey, Ma. It's me. I'm going to the store. Need anything? Milk? Bread?' Yeah. Like that.

9

So now you tell me I can't do that. You're taking away my rights. My right to talk. (pause) My right to talk wherever and whenever I want to!

Okay. I get it. You'll let me talk. Only not on my car phone. Not here. Over in the next town. Maybe. You're asking me what? What did I do before I bought this phone? (pause) Well...okay. I'll tell you what I did. I missed out on things. No, I didn't know it. I didn't have a phone in my car but nobody else did either! So it was okay to miss things. Get it? (pause)

I want you to know you're pushing civilization back about a hundred years. Maybe more. I just hope you can live with that. You do this to everybody and where will we be? We'll just have to figure out another way to get where we're going, that's all. Or...yeah...like you say...not talk at all in your town. (pause)

But, hey. Here's the thing. How'm I gonna get to use up the 1400 minutes I've got free for this month, huh? You tell me, okay? How'm I gonna do that?

Janice reveals the dark secrets of her life.

ON A WHITE HORSE

When we were kids there was this idea that the right man would come riding by on a white horse and he would find you…like magic…You'd get married right away and live happily ever after.

So when I met Gerry, I knew. I just knew. We'd get married and be happy all the time.

(pauses, looks down at her hands).

Gerry used to tell people we were crazy in love. I was always a little bit embarrassed when he said that. But I guess it was true all right. We'd go to the movies and hold hands, or maybe go dancing. Gerry loved to dance. He'd hold me close and twirl me around fast, pretending he didn't notice everybody watching. Even later on. Even when things were…different…(pause) we'd go dancing sometimes.

The first time he hit me, I thought I was dreaming. It hurt. But the worst hurt was…it was him doing the hurting. Why? I asked myself, holding a chunk of ice against my cheek while my fingers trembled with the pain…(pause) Why? (pause) Scrambling to pick up the bloody towels, racing to hide them in the washer before the kids came home.

I'd like to tell you it never happened again. But I'd be lying. It happened. I didn't count the times it happened. (pause) I tried to think. I tried to plan. Planning makes you feel you're doing something. What was I going to do? Pull the kids out of school? Tell them they'd better know right now that they could never go to college because their father…their father…
hit me sometimes.

I called my girl friend Mona. You know how sometimes when something happens it makes you feel better when you can talk about it?

11

I knew I wasn't going to tell her the truth. I was going to make up a story about a friend and how all this happened to a friend.

I didn't want to shame him, if you can believe me. And...maybe I didn't want her to think 'Poor Francey.' I had it all planned out and then when she picked up the phone I said, 'Mona, there's somebody at my door. I'll call you back.' And I never called. (pause)

I began to try to save a little, out of housekeeping money. I thought I could maybe take a secretarial course or something. The truth is I was planning to leave him. It went against everything I was ever taught, but I didn't see how I could go on living like that. I was going to try to take the course and look for a job and then I would leave. I didn't know what I was going to do about the kids...I hoped they'd come with me, but I didn't know. I knew I wasn't thinking clearly.

And then, (pause) Gerry had a stroke. It was a small one, but it was a stroke all the same. 'Of course you'll want him in a nursing home,' the doctor said. 'Oh, no. I couldn't possibly. I'll take care of him myself,' I said. I don't know why I said that. I don't know why I felt that way. (pause)

At first he couldn't do anything for himself. I had to move him and feed him and dress him and oh, you know, just everything. In a way I liked taking care of him. I liked the feeling that he needed me, that I was helping him. But I was so tired. (pause)

I began to have strange dreams. Dreams of dying...like a flower. One minute I was a bright yellow flower. Brilliant. Like the sun. Then I faded and was gone. I had the same dream over and over and over. I tried to count the dreams. It seemed important to count them. But I couldn't. I tried. But I couldn't...And I was so terribly tired. But I couldn't sleep...and the dreams began again...the same dreams...of tall flowers dying...over...and over...and over. (pause)

Then, one morning, he hit me. I was leaning over his bed, smoothing the covers, when here comes a fist at me, wham bam. I couldn't believe it, to tell the truth. I felt like hitting him back, right there in the bed. But he was a sick man, after all, and I had my health...even if I didn't feel just right. (pause)

I walked out in the hall slowly. Everything was blurry around me...and my legs didn't want to hold me up...and there was an awful feeling in my chest...and I wanted to say please...I don't feel just right. I was so tired and Gerry was screaming...I crumpled and fell and everybody ran. (pause)

I don't know what made him the way he was. I think about it. But I'll never know. All I want to say is be smart. Be strong. Run away before the dreams begin. Run away fast...before you fade away (pause) like me.

Claire instructs. She speaks directly to the audience, patiently sharing.

THE ONE

Take it slow I tell her. Smile a lot. Like this. I show her (she smiles, sweetly, slowly). One sentence at a time. Then smile. Slowly (she smiles again, demonstrating).

Wait for them to clap. (pause) Sure they will. Of course they will. You're up there. You're waiting. You're smiling at them. They know what they're supposed to do. Put their hands together and...Right. Now again. Nice and slow. That's good. That's good. That's very good. Now remember – that's no brain trust out there. It's people. Just people. Give them a chance. They want to like you. They need to like you. They're looking for a hero and you may be THE ONE, I tell you. You may be IT. (pause)

I tell her. And I tell her. And I tell her again. She's getting it. She's getting better. But oh my God so s-l-o-w-l-y.

I could do it upside down. Standing on my head. Blindfolded. Shackled. (gesture) But she's the one. Not me. Oh, yeah. Nearly forgot the clothes. Keep it simple I tell her. Look good but not too good. Someplace between Vogue and The Inquirer. And the hair. Simple. Neat. That's it. Forget glamour. Forget everything. Watch the teleprompter. But smile while you're doing it. (pause) Hey, listen. I'm not the speechwriter. I'm only the coach. She's the one. I'm the last link before the big test. I prep her for the public. I urge her on. I push-pull her through it. 'Come on!' I say over and over. 'You can do it. Yes you can! Yes you can!'

And she can. She will. Eventually. I hope. Hey, this is my job here. I get paid to do this. But oh migod...I watch her and I suffer. I watch her work through it over and over...So carefully. So painfully. And I see myself out there. Not her. Me.

14

Head up. Shoulders back. Smile, baby, smile. I would be terrific! And you'd love me. All of you. I'd make you love me. (pause) But I'm not the one. I'm not running for anything. I'm not looking for your vote ladies and gentlemen. I'm only the coach. She's the one.

BUT I WOULD BE SO GOOD! I'm a natural! Why can't they see that? Why don't they know that? Maybe they can't hear me. Maybe I need to tell them…Look. Forget her. CHOOSE ME! CHOOSE ME! I'M THE ONE!

Patty takes a chance, maybe...

I'M GOING TO MARRY WALLY MAYBE

I'm going to marry Wally. I guess. I mean he's really nice, Wally. And I really do love him. (pause) And I'm scared. (pause)

I was engaged before...and it wasn't okay...I mean...It wasn't the way it's supposed to be. (pause) And then...right away I met Wally. And he's oh...he's really nice. (pause)

You ever think how funny life can be? (pause) You ever think how really funny? I mean here I am one day all broken up...sort of...And then right away I meet Wally and the sun comes out! I mean *just like that*! And he's...oh he's...he loves me.

He's a little older than me, Wally, but that's okay. My mom...my mom she always says to marry somebody older. Somebody dependable. 'Let him take care of you' and like that...(pause)

But I don't know...You're not supposed to do that. I mean what about independence? What about being strong? What about standing out there on your own two feet? And like that?

He's a little older, Wally. I told you? (pause) I think I need somebody older. Somebody that likes to make decisions and all...I'm not too strong on that, decisions. (pause)

I was at his house yesterday. He wants me to get to know his kids and all. (pause) I don't think they like me...(pause) And the house...it's awful. I mean you can't believe how awful...you can't walk around. Wally says forget it. We'll call a service...or something. He just wants us to get married and be happy all the time.

He's so strong and confident. I never had any confidence. I took a course once. 'How to Love Yourself.' But that's a lot of garbage. How can you love yourself...when you know you're nothing? (a small laugh)

16

I tell him all the time. I'm really nothing. (pause) He doesn't believe me. Or maybe...maybe he really does believe me...and he's faking it, y'know. To make me feel good. (she turns, glances off, then slowly) Or something. (pause)

I don't think Wally's going to show. (pause) I think maybe...maybe he changed his mind. (pause) He thought about it...and he figured it could never work. (pause) I was engaged before. I was really young. He took a job out of town. It didn't seem right to leave my mother. (in a kind of desperation) She thinks I'm looking for a father...somebody to look after me...and love me...and keep me from harm! (fighting tears she begins to move off)

When you see Wally...you tell him, okay? Just tell him...tell him...I...I understand...All right? You...you tell him for me...okay...?

(she runs off, weeping, her hands covering her face)

Taylor shares a BIG secret.

HOW TO BE REALLY REALLY RICH

I went to one of those things. Those things where they take your money and they talk at you and they tell you how really easy it is to get to be really really rich.

Hey! I'll try that! Why not? That's what it's all about. Right? Give up the old 9-5, 8-4, whatever. Give it up before it gives you up. Retire. See the world...(pause)

So I go. I listen. I write it all down. That doesn't take too long, to be honest. It's a dead secret. But I'm going to tell it to you. Right now.

Two words. BUY PROPERTY. Okay, three words, BUY REAL ESTATE. That's it. (pause) Well, sure. You've got to be smart. Find the right place to buy. Get it at the right price. Find a bank that loves you. That's important. (pause)

I go running around to the banks. I'm running and I'm looking like they tell you. I'm looking at property. I'm looking at old rundown apartment houses and three family houses that used to be...once upon a time...sitting on a nice quiet street with trees and everything...and now the trees are gone and the street is filled with upside down trash cans and broken down cars...and the houses are still sitting there. (pause)

18

I look at new places. Mucho moolah. (she shakes her head) I look out in the country. Oh, nice. Really nice. Lots of trees. Lots of space. (pause) One problem. (pause) Maybe two problems. This is really beautiful country...with no schools...no stores...Nothing. Nada. (pause)

So. (pause) I think to myself. Here I am. Here I am in the beautiful...where am I? (pause) Do I want to be a...you know...developer? Do I even know how? (pause)

So. Okay. Back to square one. I go to a bank. Yeah. (she smiles) I find a bank that loves me and I buy a house. The only house I can like...afford...I buy this one...an old house that cries out, HELP! HELP! FIX ME UP! (pause) I fix it up. I rent it out just like they tell you...and then I buy another one.

I'm sailing along with this, feeling really really rich...and then guess what? I get hit with some kind of cockamamie special assessment from the city. One of my tenants moves out in a hurry and leaves the place a total wreck. Now there comes a big storm. The room springs a leak and a major pipe breaks someplace and now there's water everyplace it's not supposed to be! (pause)

I think seriously about bailing out of the entire mess when an idea hits me. An idea that is so outstanding I can't believe I thought it up! (pause)

I can...you know...teach people. For a few bucks I can tell everybody how I went all over...How I tried...Hey! For a few bucks more maybe I can sell them a book about how it's not so easy...after I sit down and write it, okay? Now I think I'm really on to something!

I can teach people what I know...what I learned. I can save them a whole lot of grief and they'll hand over a couple of green ones...And I'll get myself sort of medium rich! (pause)

So? For just a few bucks I can teach you all I know. Save you a whole lot of time. Maybe make myself really really rich...(pause)

Hey! Why didn't I think of this before?

Amy looks back.

YELLOW DISHES

'Take something,' my mother said. 'Take the china vase in the dining room...take the silver bowl on the buffet...take the little picture in the hall,' she pleaded, fighting for breath.
I wanted to please her. I wanted to do that, but I could not do it.

I knew just what I would take...if I could. The yellow dishes. The shiny yellow dishes with a tiny painted butterfly on the rim of each plate, each cup, each bowl. I should have gone into the kitchen right then, pulled each piece off the shelves and carried them home with me.

But I couldn't. I couldn't. That would have meant admitting to myself that my mother was dying. That soon she would be gone from me. And I couldn't. (pause)

Times were bad when I was a child. And then one surprising day my father found a new job. Suddenly there was money and my mother bought the yellow dishes. I was fascinated by the butterfly that sat on my breakfast cocoa cup and cereal bowl and appeared again like magic at lunch and at supper if I cleaned my plate. (pause)

'Take something,' my mother whispered painfully. But I didn't. I couldn't. I should have saved that part of my childhood. Of my past. Of my mother. But I could not do that. (pause)

My stepmother has the yellow dishes now. I've tried to tell her what they mean to me. I've tried to ask her for them. It's not easy, but I have tried.

21

Today I ask her again.

'Oh I know,' she smiles at me. 'They are pretty, aren't they? So bright. So cheerful. I gave them to my daughter. I know you understand. But, oh, wait here...'

She hands me a small cracked bowl with a faded butterfly on the rim.

'I saved this for you,' she says.

'Okay,' I tell her... 'Thanks.'

I take it in my hand and I begin to cry.

Melinda has a gift she doesn't want.

A REALLY GOOD LISTENER

Look at me. Please. Really look. I'm pretty normal. Right. (she gestures) Body. Head, Person. Okay? But I want to tell you what I really am. What I really am is a person full of secrets. Other people's secrets.

People tell me things. They love to tell me things. I don't honestly understand it. I guess I'm a really good listener...which is supposed to be a good thing. But...trust me here...it's something I don't need. (pause)

I used to think it was some kind of a true compliment when somebody whispered something they never told a living soul until now. I used to clutch the secret to myself and feel...Oh, you know...really good about the way they'd trust me with stuff about their lives. But now it's got so I don't even want to go to lunch with a friend.

Somebody asks me to lunch I just know they want to lay something high level on me and make me swear right then I'll never tell a living soul...(pause)

Look. Who do you know that walks down the aisle of the supermarket, looking for chili peppers all over the place and a strange woman clutches at my arm and whispers, 'I just left my husband. I had to tell somebody.' (pause) Why me?

Maybe I go over to Rennie's. Maybe Mike's home, okay? He's a good guy. But now there's this secret. So I'm afraid to talk to him. Maybe I'll be saying, 'No, thanks' to a glass of wine and 'Oh, sure' to a chunk of cheese and he'll know right off that by about July fifteenth he'd better be doing some serious thinking about his life. (pause)

See...Rennie's leaving him. July fifteenth. She's got this deadline in her head and now it's stuck in mine. So how can I go

23

over there when all the time I'm sitting on their couch I'm ready to...to...burst?

Sharon's off the pill. She wants a baby and Dan's really going to be surprised. Terri's husband's having an affair. He doesn't know she knows. And surer than hell he doesn't know I know. Hey. It's a secret! (pause)

I am so weighed down with it. With all of it. I feel like I'm carrying this huge back pack...Lugging around about a ton of other people's lives. Afraid I might mess up – which will definitely happen because I am on overload and I just know I'm going to forget whose secret is which.

Look. I worry. I feel responsible. (a sigh) I guess that's why everybody tells me things. They know I'm not going to blab. (a pause, she looks at the audience directly) Oh. Migod. I've been sooo good...And now I've gone and told you! Oh Migod. You're not going to tell, are you? You wouldn't, would you? You won't...will you? You'd never do that. (a pause, then carefully) Would you?

(She waits a moment, anxious, hopeful)

A young mother sits on the floor of an empty room. Near her are several small bundles of children's clothing. Absently she picks up a small shirt, a sweater, folds them, unfolds them, folds them again.

CHANCE LIGHT SNOW

I dreamt about a woman who . . . drowned her children. Her husband left her . . she didn't know what to do. (pause) She bundled them up in their good warm jackets so they wouldn't be cold . . . and she put them in the car . . . and she drove to the pond.

It was snowing. Pretty white stuff coming down and down. She thought it would melt . . .but it kept coming faster . . .and faster . . .and faster . . .

She got out of the car to look at the snow. And the car . . .the car . . .went into the pond. The children were crying and then it was quiet. She saw Robbie's red shoulder and Danny's blue arm. She called out to them.

'Robbie!' she called. 'Danny! Mommy's here! Mommy's here!'

But it was quiet. (pause) Bad boys. They heard. But they didn't make a sound. Not . . .a sound . . .(pause) Bad boys. (pause)

I was a child once. My mother took care of me. Washed me. Dressed me. Fed me. Poor Mommy. How did she do that? How did she do that every day? All alone . . .only the children. No one to love. No one to laugh with. No one to be pretty for . . .(absently she picks up something from the heap of clothing, puts it down) Do you hear them . . ? Crying . . ? I thought I heard . . .something. It's the snow maybe. It's still snowing . . .And my dream. My terrible dream (pause) Where is he? Why did he leave us? Where did he go? (long pause)

I cried. The children cried. I cried because he left. They cried because I cried. And they were hungry. Poor babies.

25

I sat on the floor and I played with them. I sang for them. I clapped my hands and I sang for them and I told them it was a party.

'Clap your hands! Sing a song! It's a party!' I said. But they were hungry. They cried and cried. I didn't know what to do. (pause)

I put on their jackets and went for a ride. (long pause) It started to snow. Pretty white snow. I wanted to show them the pretty white snow. (abruptly she snatches a piece of small clothing from the bundle and slowly begins to tear it into small strips)

He told me he loved me. He told me! HE told me he'd be with me always. And then he . . .he went away. He went away and he never came back. I wanted to hurt him . . .(she rises suddenly, dropping the torn bits of fabric to the floor) He'll be sorry, won't he? He'll be sorry. But it's too late. I'll tell him! I'll tell him! It's too late! (long pause) And it's all your fault.

I went to the pond. It was snowing . . .(she glances desperately at the stark and empty room) I went to the pond. (pause) I went to the pond . . .I WANTED TO HURT YOU! I WANTED TO PUNISH YOU! They're gone . . .And it's all your fault . . .

Annie Parris, swinging an old leather flying helmet and a pair of goggles in her hand, describes her life.

WHAT AM I BID?

They tried to sell my stuff the other day. Even had an auction. Fan-cy. Couldn't get rid of a damn thing. (she laughs) It's the God's truth. Nobody wanted anything. Not anything of mine for sure. (pause) Somebody parted with a few bucks for an old envelope with Orville Wright's name on it. I seem to remember writing him a letter one time . . .I was looking for a job.

I was pretty damn good, you know. But this must've been one of those times when I got tired of hustling air-struck . . . (a shrug) what d'ya call them . . .? Thrill seekers . . .I guess . . .All kinds. All sizes. All ages. All of them looking for something 'different,' something 'challenging,' to do on a Saturday afternoon from one to four.

'Challenging' . . .(she grins) It's really kinda funny you know. They'd buy a ticket for a buck, put on the extra helmet I always brought along, climb into the cockpit with me . . .I'm doing everything. The thinking . . .the planning . . .the flying . . .And they're sitting in back. Nice, all cozy . . .being challenged! (she laughs)

Yeah (pause) People are funny and thank God for it. Because I could make a living doing what I loved. Not a big living. But a living. (pause)

This one time . . .a clear sunny afternoon. . .there was a crowd up at the far tend of the field. I saw them from where I was getting ready to land. I couldn't imagine what all the whoop and holler was about, y'know. I came, nice and slow . . .brought her down just perfectly. (she grins) Okay. Maybe I was showing her off. A bit.

27

I climbed out and walked over to where the crowd was circling around the prettiest little Piper Cub and standing next to her, the handsomest guy I had ever seen . . .Head thrown back, talking a mile a minute to whoever would listen . . .And I've got to tell you that crowd was listening. It seemed like they couldn't get enough of him. Wham . . .Slam . . .I felt the same myself.

'Annie Parris, what the devil's the matter with you?' I asked myself. 'You've never seen a pilot before?' (pause)

We were married twelve years. (pause) Before he . . .crashed. (pause) There were a whole lot of crashes in those days. You . . .you almost kind of expected it. You . . .(pause) you just didn't know when it was going to happen (pause) I kept on flying . . .But it wasn't the same. I even got married again . . .after a while. That wasn't the same either. But I was lonely . . .and he was kind. (pause) So now there's this auction. Stupidest thing I've ever heard. I had a helluva life. But nobody knows me now. Nobody wants my stuff.

But my life? Oh boy! If I could sell my life would somebody buy it? Would somebody want to live it?

I'll bet they would. *I'll just bet they would!*

(Confident, she walks off.)

Boston. 1967. Dedicated to Kathy S. She ran the race:

A woman in dark sweats runs onstage, runs in place briefly, turns to the audience.

BREAKING THE TAPE

There's this guy where I work . . . He's out there running on the street on his lunch hour, ducking the traffic, training for the marathon, quote, unquote. He doesn't know what he's doing. Trust me. But he can run the marathon, if he makes it, and I can't . And I'm good. Believe me, I'm good!

I love to run. Get out there and just let go. Run in the morning. Run at night. It's all good and beautiful. If you grew up where I did you'd probably feel the same. Every year there's this huge event. A marathon run. Everybody lined up all along the route, watching and cheering. I was two years old the first time I watched. Two years old. . .in a stroller . . .yelling my head off for Johnny Kelley. That's what they tell me anyway.

Now I run for fun. And I'm pretty good. Hell, I'm damn good. I know how to run. I know how to pace myself. I run after work . On weekends. I've got good strong legs and I know how to use them. The thing about the marathon, it's for men. Men only. Just men. Believe it. They named it for someplace in Greece where the men used to run a special race every year. So I guess that's why the idea of a woman running the marathon is a great big no-no. And does that ever make me mad.

I'm out here every year, same spot on the route. I'm out there waving and cheering and every year I think – that's me. That's me slogging past, sweat on my face, a wet rag on my head, pushing for the tape.

29

And every year I know it's not, and it's never going to be. Unless . . .unless. . .I get the idea I'm training for the marathon. It can't happen, but I train anyway. I pace myself. I start running for distance. Twenty-six miles with hills. It's a tough run. So? I just might try it. In your dreams, I tell myself.

But one bright Saturday, early in the A.M. I'm out there on my solo run and the dream I've been fighting back comes up and smacks me in the face so hard it stops me. I stand there on the road and I know right then I'm going to do it. I don't care what happens. I'm going to do it. I'm going to run the marathon. I find the toughest places, hills, ditches, whatever. I run in the rain. I run in the snow. I build up my endurance until twenty-six miles begins to seem like almost nothing. And then I start to work on the real problem. Like how can I get myself in the run? Clothes are easily. Dark sweats and a cap with my hair shoved underneath. Getting in the race is the real challenge, tougher than the run. But I have a plan.

Comes the big day. I hide in the woods near the starting point, maybe a quarter mile down the road. I wait for a few of the early runners to pass by and then I slip out to join them. I'll be disqualified right there if anyone notices me. But I'm not out to win. I'm not doing this to steal a medal. I'm doing it for me. And it's about time.

I find my rhythm. Beautiful. A little faster. No, too fast. Better slow down. A long stretch ahead. Here come the hills. Good thing I trained for hills . . .I'm in a crowd. . .Drop back. . .Okay. Move on. People cheering. Ye Gods! Little kids. Somebody dashes out. . .Hands me a lemon. I rub it on my face, the back of my neck. Whoa, boy. Somebody's watching me. An official. Here he comes . . .Right on my tail. Push faster. Try to lose him. . .There's the finish line! God it's hot!

30

He's inches in back of me. . .Hit it! Hit it! Now! Pull off the cap. . .Who cares what he says . .I'm illegal . . .It doesn't count . . .SO WHAT!

I did it! And they know! I ran the marathon. I did it for me. And does it feel good? YOU BETCHA!

She stands in front of the audience as at a podium, energetic and determined.

THE CLUB

Okay, folks. Okay. It's *time*. You've had four long years to think about it. *Four long years.* So who is it? Who's it gonna be? (pause)

This club holds an election every four years. No matter what! It's in the by-laws. The by-laws. by . . .la. . .w. . .s. . . RIGHT? And it's time. It's time already! We have to come up with somebody! We have to have a *candidate* . . . (pause)

Remember? The last time we did this was four years ago AND WE WERE GREAT! WE WERE AWESOME! WE HAD CANDIDATES COMING OUT OF THE KAZOO! (pause)

So what is this, hey? What's going on? (patiently) We *need* to do this, people. We do this or we change the old by laws. OKAY? We change them over to say *nobody wants the job*. It's a dirty job and nobody loves you no matter what you try to do. The members don't appreciate you. And your husband or your wife, as the case may be, complains all the time that they never see you . . .And when they do get to see you you're huddled up with Charlie here trying to figure out what to do next that'll make everybody love you.

So what about me? Your better half asks. Don't I matter? Don't I go to the wall for you? Don't I smile until my face hurts? Don't I shake a lot of hands? Don't I do all that for you?

Well now the truth is you do it for THE CLUB! Say it right out now. THE CLUB, THE CLUB, THE CLUB, I DO IT FOR THE CLUB! (she waits)

There you go! Don't you feel better now? So come on! Stand up and be counted! You there, Peg! Or Jerry? *Great hair Jerry!* Sam? *Love that smile!* (she waits briefly) COME ON! COME ON! We need you. We need SOMEBODY!

WE NEED SOMEBODY TO BE THE PRESIDENT! And look, I promise you . . . you won't have to do a thing. Charlie'll take care of everything. . .like always. He'll tell you what to do . He'll fill you in. He'll be right there fixing up. . *everything*...

So come on, folks...Come on...WE NEED YOU! And all you have to do is stand up here and smile f'Godsake! You don't need to do a thing. Not one itty bitty *thing!* (pause) Charlie'll do everything . . . like always.

She is limited and brave.

A BIG FISH

I am sitting inside of something that moves in the sky. Like a big fish. Only in the sky. I am sitting near a place where I can see things. I can see big soft white things. Like clouds maybe. Or beds for babies. Only there are no babies out there.

I think there's a baby in here someplace. I can hear that noise that babies make. But I can't see a baby anyplace. I turn myself around and I look every place. But I can't see a baby.

Maybe I'm, dreaming about a baby. I like to dream. When I dream I'm like other people. Nobody looks at me funny when I dream. Some people are sitting near me. One is next to me. I see them looking funny at me. They think I don't know . . . Inside myself I am just like them. But they don't know that.

There is a big tag pinned on me. Like on a suitcase. Or a dog. (pause) A dog is nice. A dog can eat and pee and crap. I can do all those things. (pause) A dog can bark. Barking is talking for a dog. Talking is for people.

I can't talk. I try. But what comes out is more like sounds. Big sounds. Little sounds. Some people can figure out what I want to say. But most people can't. Maybe they don't try enough. Or something.

The people sitting near me . . . they look at me funny. I see them looking at me funny. (pause) Inside my head I am just like them. But they don't know. They look at me and they see a round person in a pink dress with a big tag pinned in front and they thing to themselves, Oh, that is not me.

That could never be me. I could never be like that. I am tall and strong and beautiful. I know what they think. I know. But they don't know what I think. And that's all right. I like it that I can look at everybody and think what I want.

34

They would maybe laugh if they knew what I was thinking. But that's all right. (pause) That's all right with me. (pause) Because I can't say anything and that is what keeps me out of trouble.

She enters slowly, with obvious pain, then carefully moves into a waiting chair.

ANGIE-WHERE-SHE-IS-IN-LIFE

I know you're wondering how I got like this. (pause, a small laugh) It could be anything, couldn't it? An accident? A crime? (small pause) It wasn't any of those things. The truth is...I did it to myself. (pause) You're surprised, aren't you? Are you more surprised that I did it? Or that I'm telling you...what happened...? (pause) I was young. I fell in love. I thought it was love... Maybe it was. There's no way I could know...to be honest.

I'd hardly been near a boy. Except for him. Donny. (pause) I come from a very strict family. My father is the head of the family. He makes the rules. I can't remember my father praising anyone. Perhaps a small smile for my mother if his dinner pleases him...Or for me...if I laugh at one of his jokes about the Mafia. (a rueful smile) My father is famous for his Mafia jokes. (pause)

My father runs a business. He works hard, but he likes that. He says he has good help. One of his helpers is a woman, Anna. I'll...I'll get to that. First I...I want to tell you about Donny. I had sex with Donny. I loved him so. I couldn't help myself. It was a sin. I knew it was a sin. Sex outside of marriage is a sin. But I didn't care. I couldn't help myself. All the while I knew it was a sin. And I knew my father would find out. I knew that. I don't know how. I just knew. And I was so frightened. I couldn't sleep. I couldn't eat. All I could think of was Donny and what my father would do to me if he found out...when he found out.

Donny wanted to marry me. I didn't know what to do. I really did not know what to do.

36

I wanted to run away with Donny. I wanted to stay home with my mother. I wanted to be like anybody else.
I wanted to be what I was…
One day I got brave. I still didn't understand it. It wasn't at all like me…I dressed myself carefully and went to see my father at his office. I had a little speech prepared. I was going to tell him about Donny and how we loved each other and we wanted to be married and that I wanted his blessing…his approval…

I was so nervous, so scared. I rushed into his office and there he was. With Anna. She smoothed down her skirt and buttoned her blouse and smiled up at me like she'd been smiling ever since I could remember. And my father got very busy doing something at his desk…And my head was pounding…and my neck was trembling…and my skin felt like fire…I ran to the window…and I threw it open…And I jumped.

(pause)

I landed on the roof.
I was a mess. But I was alive.
Alive and nothing accomplished.

Everything was the same.
Nothing had changed.
Except for my pain.
I live at home now. I work for my father. You probably wonder how I can do that…how I can bear to be with him.
But it doesn't really matter. Nothing matters much anymore.

(pause)

37

Sometimes I think about the girl I was...And would you believe...some days I can't think why. I can't go back to the terror that drove me...

It was as though I lived in a huge room surrounded by doors. The walls were doors. The windows were doors. And every door I tried was the same. I was on the first floor of a house. A strange house. And every door opened to nothing. To blackness and emptiness. I ran around the room opening doors and closing them, opening doors and closing them, until finally I opened the last door... And I jumped and I thought, well all right now...it's over, it's over. I'm free. And (pause)...I woke up...and here I am. (long pause)

It was hard at first. But it was only my body that struggled. My mind was free. I couldn't think. I didn't have to think. There was nothing to think about. How to walk. How to move. That was nothing.

The hard part...the really hard part...that was over. Finished. The blackness gone...and here I am. Broken. Living. I don't think about Donny much anymore. He's part of my past. A big part. But past.

He has a wife. Two little girls. (pause)
Would I change anything? If I could? Sometimes I think I might have tried to be braver. To tough it out. But the way I was...I don't honestly think I could.
I did the only thing I could think of at that moment and it turned out...funny.
I'm a joke.
I'm one of my father's jokes.
His best joke.
I'm alive.

Herbie's Mom confides

SAY HELLO TO MY DAUGHTER

On the day my son became my daughter...I wept. My body shook until I thought it would break in pieces. My eyes burned from salt tears. My throat was on fire. I wept alone all that day...and when the sun went down and the day was gone I wiped my eyes. I combed my hair.

I opened my door and I called out in a voice I never knew I had... 'ALL RIGHT!' I called. 'ALL RIGHT! LET'S CELEBRATE!'

That's what we're going to do, Herbie, I tell him in my heart. No choices now. This is it, Herbie...this is it.

Do any of you remember him? My son...Herbie...? He was the sweetest...the dearest...the best son...the best son anyone could wish for. And he *tried*. He tried so. I miss him. I miss him every damn day. But he's gone. But he's gone. He's gone and he's never coming back.

I have a daughter now. I always wanted a daughter. And now she's here with me.

We do things together...my daughter and I. We talk. We do things. Only sometimes...sometimes you know...sometimes maybe we'll be having lunch together at a pretty restaurant...and maybe I'll look across the table at her...my new daughter...and I'll look again...and I'll kind of blink, you know...and I'll wonder to myself...Where is my boy? Where is my Herbie? Where did he go? But I don't say anything.

I smile across the table. I pick up my sandwich. I drink my coffee. And all the time, I'm thinking...thinking...WHY? WHY HERBIE? WHY? TELL ME WHY!

INTERVIEW WITH THE MOTHER

I know why you're here. But I can't talk to you. I can't talk to anybody. You can talk to my husband. He's not like me. He can talk about it. He talks to everybody. He likes that, talking.

He can't talk to me. I cover my ears. I cover my ears and I run from the room and I look for a place to hide myself and there isn't any place like that. If I hide in the bed I think about it. If I walk in the yard I think about it. If I go to the car I begin to scream. Not outside, but inside myself. Like bleeding. Like I am bleeding inside.

My son was always a little bit different. A little bit not exactly what you might think. I pretended to myself not to know. Maybe if I didn't know, it was not that way.

So now I sit and I think. I turn my thoughts this way and that way, like something I hold in my two hands, and I work them around and around. She was a pretty girl. A pretty girl with a pretty smile. Did she smile at him? In school maybe? When she was on the street laughing with her girl friends? Did she give him a reason to think that she liked him?

He is shy with girls, my son. Quiet. Uncomfortable. Or so I thought watching him. But what do I know? What does a mother know about her child? Deep inside?

There were things I saw, but I didn't see. There was the cat. The children's cat, next door. They hunted all over for the cat and they found it, dead in the cellar. Our cellar. How did it get there? To this day I don't know. My son said it crawled in the window and starved itself to death. But the window was locked and the cat's throat was cut. I saw that for myself, but I said nothing. What I thought I buried deep inside myself and I kept quiet.

And now they come to us from the television, from the newspapers, from the radio. I say nothing. I bite my tongue to say nothing. I am nice. I am quiet. But inside I am screaming.

40

How could this happen? How could he do this? How could he do this...this...unspeakable thing?

Because he did it. I know. I know. He doesn't have to tell me. I know. And I feel...I can't tell you how I feel. I want to hurt him for this. Some days I wake up and I think it would be right if I would kill him. Yes, I think that. And then I think he is mine He is my son. I made him this way. And the thought is more than I can bear and so I think no, never mind, why him? I should kill myself. This is me. This is all me. Somehow I did this thing through him. And then I think he is a sick boy and I should try to save him. He did this thing like a baby that doesn't know what it is doing and I am the mother and I must save him. And then I think of that girl and I think of her mother and I lock my heart and I say nothing.

I got to see him in that place. That place where they keep people who do such things. I look at his face, his eyes, his hands. He turns his face away from me. I think he's afraid of what I might see in his face. In his eyes. I look at him and I make myself think of the boy he was, the boy who never once forgot my birthday. I talk to him. I save little things to tell him, foolish jokes. Little things. I smile and I talk and when the time is up and they take him away I go into the toilet where nobody can hear and I cry until my face is hot and there are no more tears.

And then I get on the bus and I go home and I fix supper for my husband. (pause)

This is what I think. I think he was ashamed. He had to do it because he was ashamed. He was ashamed of what he had done to her and so he had to fix it so she could never tell. That is what I think.

But what do I know? Nothing. Let me tell you. *Nothing.* You think you know your child? Your own child? You think you know what he is really like? Let me tell you, you don't know. You can't know. Nobody knows anybody. *Nobody. Never.*

41

Maybe he's not our son. Maybe there was a mix-up at the hospital when he was born. This can happen. I told that to my husband. Maybe he's a mistake. Maybe he's not our son. But my husband, he's not like me. He looks at things straight in the eye. 'We don't deserve this,' he said. 'But he is our son. And there is nothing we can do.'

I dream that it is morning and somebody wakes me to say this is all a horrible mistake. It never happened. The girl is alive, a smile on her mouth, her hair wild in the wind, and my son is beside me, and the world is good.

But I know. I know. That is the dream and the other is all that is real. And the other is what I must live with until the day they put me in the ground.

Louise's elderly mother has recently died in a nursing home. Louise confides her feelings.

CUSTARD

She didn't know me…toward the end.
She didn't know who I was…
(long pause)
I ran to the Home every day.
Morrie was furious. But I…I couldn't
Seem to help myself.
And all the time I kept thinking…
I'm going to lose my mother. And when you lose your mother…
You're nobody. You're nothing.

(a silence)
One morning I walked in with some custard I'd made.
I was very tired. I'd hardly slept at all…worrying about her…
She opened her eyes slowly…and looked right at me and said,
'Who are you? Do I know you?'
I…I didn't want to upset her…So I told her who I was, very quietly, trying to hide the way I felt…
'I'm Louise. Your daughter. Louise,' I said.
'I'm Louise, Mamma…'
She just looked at me in a funny way and laughed,
Sort of…and said, 'You're trying to fool me. Why are you trying to fool me? You can't be my daughter. My daughter is young…and beautiful. Who are you, old lady?'
(long pause)
She…She wouldn't eat the custard, either.
She…thought it was poisoned.

Reena enters briskly, carrying a large notebook. She flips through the pages efficiently then, smiling brightly, she moves to face the audience.

 REAL ESTATE

All right. (she closes the notebook) We are here today for one reason. We are going to tour this magnificent mansion. You've all heard the sad story. And you've each been asked to put down a small deposit in order to...well...yes...But a thousand dollars is not very much when you consider this magnificent mansion.

Quite frankly my firm...We are number one, but of course you know that...My firm felt that in order to attract serious buyers and only serious buyers we should...
Well...frankly...we wanted to eliminate lookers
and the simply curious.

So. Now. We are going to examine this magnificent structure. (she waves an arm in a large vague gesture) Fourteen bedrooms, twenty baths. Twenty and a half baths if you count the little half in the garage. Now. Please admire the gorgeous entrance hall. Observe the marble inlay on the walls...imported from Italy. The mosaics on the ceiling...(she gestures, grandly, at the ceiling) Archers, wolves and birds of prey. (she opens her notebook hastily, examines it) Hmm...Look. (she puts down the notebook) I'm going to level with you. (she takes a deep breath)

The owner...of this magnificent mansion is...in jail. For fraud. His partner disappeared. His wife ran away. To Switzerland, maybe. Nobody actually knows where she is. I'm supposed to sell this...oversized...palazzo...so all the people he owes money to...and they do make up a rather impressive list...so they can get paid.

But...there are some problems. The first problem is...Can anyone tell me...? (she waits, hopeful) Well. The first problem is...Who wants it? Who can afford to live like this? Who can pay the taxes, for one thing? Who has the...the...wherewithal, if I may say so...to...uh...staff it? Clear the impressive curving private driveway? Manicure the lush and lovely lawns? See to the tennis courts and pools? Yes, there are actually three pools – one in, two out.

You see where this is going, don't you? WE ARE STUCK. Well, not our firm exactly. But the bank. Actually there are several banks involved... And the little people. It's always the little people, am I right?

So I said to my boss, 'Who wants it?' And he said, believe this...He said... 'Reena, you're creative. Come up with somebody.' So I came up with you and here we all are.
(she laughs)

The...uh...prior owner...cheated everybody. He cheated everybody in sight. He took their cash and eh built this...pile. So now, if they're really lucky, they'll get back three cents on a dollar. Okay, maybe four. Five cents the most.

Can you even imagine somebody doing this? Can you see him sitting down after breakfast...two fried eggs, a date muffin, coffee with cream... We know a lot about this guy. Actually we know all about him, except where he hid the money. So now he's sitting down after breakfast digesting his eggs, etcetera and it comes to him. A really great idea, if he can get away with it. It's pretty complicated. But basically he figured out a way to sell a whole lot of property he didn't own. Nobody owned it. It wasn't there. It didn't exist. He cheated everybody and then he took the cash and built this...this...(pause)

You know, I've got to tell you. I thought being in real estate would be fun. Dress up. Get out of the house. Meet lots of people. Make a few bucks. Everybody's always telling me I've got a zippy personality. And it's all personality, selling.

So here I am. Nobody's going to buy this place. Of course if they do, I'll get a nice fat commission which will get

45

split up about a zillion ways. But I'm never going to sell it. I can't keep a straight face. Twenty and a half bathrooms. My God. Every time I say it I have a fit. Did he have bad kidneys? Or was he maybe trying to wash off the blood, like somebody out of Shakespeare? And did it bother him, stealing people's money away from them? Or did it make his eggs taste better, thinking he was smarter than anybody else?

I'd like to ask him that, If I ever have a chance. I'd like to know. I really would. I'd like to see him squirm.

He's got some of your money...(she points to the audience) and your money (she points again) and my money.

Oh, yes. He's got my money, too. I'm in real estate. Right? And I believed him. (long pause) What a joke. (she picks up her notebook) Well. Thank you all for coming. I hope you learned something.

(She walks out)

Estelle looks back.

V.I.P.

I was very important. (beat) I was extremely important. (beat) They could not get along without me. They told me so. Many times. Did they believe it? I can't say now. But if they were honest they knew. They gave me a title…a small nameplate on my desk…and a small salary to match. (pause)

My girlfriend Bunny likes to remind me how it really was. She reads the business news. She calls me up and tells me all about the salaries that women are getting now…six figures…and we laugh together.

Maybe we really ought to cry – not laugh – But hey, what good would that do? So we laugh.

Laughing's good for you. There's this idea that if you laugh you live longer…or something. So we laugh. What the hell. Maybe we'll live longer. Maybe we won't. But it is funny, in a way, depending on how you look at it. 'Upside down? Or right side up?' Bunny says. And she laughs. Healing. Remembering.

There weren't a whole lot of opportunities for women in those days. When Bunny and I started in at THE COMPANY we thought we were so lucky…we were ambitious and hard-working. Just like the ads said. 'Hard-working, ambitious, go-getter wanted for this…that…the other…Good pay (don't even ask me what that meant!) and paid vacation.'

That meant five days off every year. Five days with pay. You tried to work it right around a holiday. Didn't always happen.

I was in the pool at first. (laughing) The secretarial pool, honey. Then I got promoted. Secretary to the boss of the division. And was he ever fussy! Call me up at home any old hour. Where's this? Where's that? Did I mail the confirmation to Chicago? Where were the figures from yesterday's meeting? What time was his lunch appointment with the big wheels tomorrow? (pause)

I followed him around and I learned. Got so I knew more about the job than he did. (pause) I was invaluable. They told me so. (she laughs) Invaluable…whatever that meant! (long pause)

48

So now...now I'm retired. I manage...on my pension. I don't go wild. But I manage. Now and then Bunny calls me up and reads off the financial news. Who's getting promoted...Who's moving on...who's retiring with what bonus and stock and all...

And I sit here wondering about my pension... And how is THE COMPANY doing... And will they have enough to keep on paying me... And how on this Earth am I going to manage if they can't...or don't...or won't...

Of course I don't say anything like that to Bunny. We crack jokes and laugh together about old times...

But she knows what I'm thinking. And I know she's thinking exactly the same thing.

I RAN IN THE RAIN

I ran in the rain I ran in the dark
Down the long driveway through the trees along the road.

I ran dragging my nightgown through the wet
Crazily running and crazily wishing we lived where houses were
close, where neighbors were near,
Thinking how once we lived like that, tiny houses for new
marriages, little houses for love.

I ran up the winding drive past the sweet flower beds past the
thick trees.

I pounded on the door
Who is that?
Who is that at our door?
In her thin nightgown heavy with rain?
They pulled me in
They wrapped me in blankets
They poured hot drinks into me
They were ready to call the police
The police
The police

Oh God the police
His name in the paper his reputation…in shreds
He will be so angry.
Oh God
We must, they said. We must. Just look at you.
Just look at you.
In the morning? Please, I begged. In the morning?
You must stay here tonight
Said the wife looking at her husband
Waiting for his approval, his sharing,
His…something…
Sure he said. Sure. Oh sure
I stayed
One night
In the guest room
The neat careful guest room
I sat on the bed
The tidy small bed
I tried to think
All night I tried to think
Think, mind! Think! I said
But my mind shut down on me
It refused to think for me
Morning.
They gave me food. They gave me clothes.
They called the police.
There is a shelter, they told me. A safe place.
An empty bed.
A bed for a woman escaping from something dark and terrible.
They took me there and I slept
I slept all day. And then I woke up.

This is stupid, I said
I have a home.
I'm going home. To think
I called a cab. I told the driver 'wait here.
I'll go in. I'll get some money. I'll pay you'
I went inside. He was there. I ran to the door.
He knocked me down. I got up. He hit me again.
The driver came. The police came. They brought me here…
And now I'm here
My life.
The life I thought was mine
Has run away like water on the ground
But I'm here
And I'm safe
For how long?

When LOTTIE is nervous she eats – anything. As she tells this story, her anxieties surface and she nibbles and munches as she speaks, reaching into the box of crackers she carries.

LOTTIE

I know a cute story. You want to hear a cute story?

There was this woman who liked to cook. She liked to cook for her children. She liked to cook for everybody, but really for her children. She liked to see them eat. It did her heart good, she liked to say. There was only one problem. Come a holiday or a Friday night, she would shop ahead, cook, bake, freeze, whatever. And all the time she was baking and chopping and doing she would be thinking, wouldn't it be nice if I could figure out a way to sit down with my children while they were eating. It gives me such joy to prepare for them. But why is it I can never go to the table fast enough to enjoy with them while they're eating?

So this one time she planned and she figured how she would put the soup on the table and bring the chicken and the potatoes and the vegetables and the salad and how she could have the coffee and the fruit and the cake all prepared on a tray ahead of time and how she could sit at the table and enjoy together with her children. She smiled to think of how nice it would be. So this night the children came, three grown children with their husbands and their wives. And she brought the hot soup to the table and then the chicken on a platter and the mashed potatoes and gravy and the three kinds of vegetables and the salad and the dressing. She went into the kitchen to take off her apron and see if maybe she had forgotten something when she heard a loud voice and then another and another. She ran to hear better what they were saying. 'Sit down, Ma and bring the cake!' Three times she heard that. Then she sat down, all alone, at the kitchen table and ate her dinner and let them wait.

53

Martie has a plan.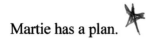

WHAT'S IN A NAME?

My name is Martha Bradley Preston. Nobody knows that for sure. I've been Martha Preston for so long. Nobody knows Martie Bradley.

I couldn't wait, you know. When I think of it...I couldn't wait to change my name to his. We went to the movies on our first date. Claudette Colbert...and...somebody. He gave me a little kiss...right on my cheek. I went straight up to my room with my coat still on and I started writing on every scrap of paper I could find. Martie Preston. Martha Preston. Mrs. Roger Preston.

I gave my name away. Well let's be honest here. I threw it away. I didn't want it anymore. I had Roger's name. My name was nothing. Something I'd outgrown, like an old sweater or a worn out pair of shoes.

Well now things are different. When my daughter went and got married she kept her name. My son's wife...well...she's got one of those complicated names for herself. She's Susan Hubbard-Preston and you better not forget it.

Well, that's all right. It just took some getting used to on my part. Like a whole lot of other things. Loud music and gas you pump yourself. Shaved heads and people sleeping on the street. Those big cars that look just like delivery vans and funny little phones that everybody seems to walk around with...not to mention kids with roller blades that scare me to pieces...

What I mean is here I am and nobody can find me. Here I am. I'm alone now. Roger's gone. And here I am. I think about my friends. Old friends. Girls I grew up with. Girls I was so close to…like Toby and Selma and Lucille.

They got married and moved away years ago. And what I'd like to know is where are they? How can I find them? How can they find me?

You're probably going to tell me 'Put an ad in the paper.' Or maybe 'hire a detective.' Or even go on the internet. I suppose I could try to do that. But what I'd really like is to pick up the phone and there's Toby. Or Selma. Or maybe Lucille. But it's not going to happen. I don't know their husbands' names and they don't have a clue about mine.

So I'm thinking. I'm thinking in my next life…Oh, sure. I'm planning on that. I need a next life to try to use all the stuff I've learned in this one. And in my next life I'm planning to be me.

I want my friends to find me. I want to know where they are. I want to open the phone book…I hope they still have phone books…I want to open it and there they are. Right there. Toby and Selma and Lucille.

Because I've lost enough and I don't want to lose any more.

Honey changes her act. She runs onstage, bouncy, cheerful, working the audience.

STAND UP/SIT DOWN

I'm thinking of a word...I need a special word to tell you what I do. If I don't tell you, you'll never guess...(she laughs) I DO LIPS! Lipology...Lipologist...THAT'S ME! That's totally me.

I take a nothing face...Hey out there! (she points to the audience) No you...(she laughs) The other one. In back of you... (pause) It's a joke. Okay? (she laughs) Yeah, you could do it yourself. You could take your lips and play around...But then where would I be? No place and starving and I like to eat. (she waits, hopeful, for applause) Well. Okay. So...uh...no more lips. (a pause) All right. Let me try something different, okay?

Let me tell you about my mom. She's...well...you know...my mom. And I think she's pretty funny, so I try it out. I tell a few jokes (a shrug) about...you know...my mom...And what y' know...that night...my luck...she's sitting right out in the audience! (she laughs)

Did I know? Am I psychic?

I complain to my dad. I tell him...Hey you know it would be kind of good if you'd like tell me she was gonna be there. So what does he say? (mimics) 'She was tryin' t' surprise you.' (pause) Yeah. Right.

She nearly surprised me right outta there.

Hey, I'm new at this. I'm trying, but this is new. Who's got writers? (a shrug) I've got me. And sometimes me doesn't cut it. Like that night.

Hey. That night my mom sits there while I kid about her and tell her old jokes to anybody that'll listen. And finally she can't stand it anymore I guess, so she gets up and tells a few herself. And what if I tell you she's funnier than me? Yeah. Well.

56

The truth is the truth. But that is not to say it makes me rip-roaring happy... (pause)

That night I can't sleep. I try out every part of the bed. The top. The bottom. About three in the A.M. I'm ready to almost crawl under the bed when it comes to me. Hear this now. A TEAM! (she gestures broadly)

Forget about trying to compete with my mom. Forget about stealing her jokes. Join up with her! Work with her! Make us a team!

I'm up early... With no sleep you can get up fast. I figured that out by myself – a new law of nature. I make coffee, toast, the works. And then I pull it out. 'Hey, Ma...What d' you say – a team?' Well, okay. She's plenty surprised. But she's game. We work out a routine. And we do it. So guess what? (pause) You guessed it. Right? They hate me. Love her. Hey, Mom! (she gestures broadly, waves offstage) I'm the opener. She's the show! (she applauds, facing off stage) PLEASE WELCOME MY MOM! (a gesture to the audience)

Mitzi's club act. She speaks directly to the audience, holding up a large APPLAUSE sign at odd moments.

MITZI RITZI

I went to look for a job. They said 'Lady, you're too old.' Too old for what? I said. I want to work, not go to bed with you. Well they didn't think that was very funny I guess. But they had me fill out one of those applications...and down at the bottom, after where it says 'experience,' it says 'age of children.'

Well I think. This is interesting. They want to give my kids a job too? So I ask them and they tell me 'we need to know how old your children are in case you're working and they need you.' Well. Here I am. Caught. Say...my kids have kids...and those kids are old enough to have kids! But I figure if I say anything they'll figure I am way too old and they'll never hire me. So I take a deep breath and as fast as I can I tell them 'Fourteen. My kids are fourteen.' 'They're both fourteen?' they say. 'Twins!' I say, 'Twins.'
(she holds up the APPLAUSE sign, laughing).

Hey, they hired me! But it didn't last. Why is it nothing good ever lasts? (pause)

Sometimes I'd like to say to life 'Hold on. Give me a minute here.' But you know that never happens. It just gets busier and busier... Kids grow up and get married and you've got a whole new set of people to get used to. And while that's happening, your roof springs a leak and the washing machine breaks down and they figure out your taxes in a whole new way... Your friends get sick and die on you. And your car goes. (pause)

Speaking of cars... Did you hear the story about the woman whose husband died and they'd been together a long time and everybody thought she'd go to pieces now he was gone? But she fooled them. She was sad. But she was okay.

58

So then, a couple of years later, her eyes got bad and they took away her driver's license. Oh, didn't she carry on! They had to give her Valium! Got to be kind of a joke. Did you bury your husband? Or bury your car? Finally somebody asks her 'How come you didn't carry on like this when your husband died?' 'Well,' she says, 'I spent a helluva lot more time with this car than I ever did with him!' (She holds up the APPLAUSE sign)

Awful, isn't it? But hey, a good laugh's worth it! (she laughs) Come back and see me! Monday nights! We'll laugh some more!
(She holds up the APPLAUSE sign again, smiling, waiting)

Mitzi looks back.

A SMALL VELVET CHAIR

My mother named me Marianne, but when I went to school, I told the kids my name was Mitzi. They'd come to the house looking for me and my mother would tell them 'there's nobody here by that name.' (she laughs)

The big treat was going downtown with my mother on a Saturday. Little white gloves and a hat. We'd have lunch in the big department store over on Main Street. We'd always order the same thing – chicken salad sandwich and strawberry ice cream soda. My mother's gone. The store's gone. Main Street is a mess, and I'm an old lady. I don't think about it much. I'd rather tell jokes. But the truth is the truth and you can't run away from it, even if you'd like to sometimes.

I used to drive my mother nuts. She'd tell me what to do, I'd do something else. You have to do that, you have to push against somebody. You have to test yourself and who else is there? Who else is going to put up with that nuttiness. Tell the truth. Who is it?

I've got a picture of my mother here someplace. When I look at my mother's face I think about, would you believe it? I think about time, of all things. I think how one minute I was trying to figure out where to put her little velvet chair that I took when she died. And there's that chair, right there, with most of the velvet worn off.

And I look at it and I think how did that happen? When did that happen? And who would believe it's been so many years since my mother went? (pause)

Sometimes I think about myself. How did I get from her to me? My friends are gone. There's hardly anybody left that knows what I think, what I feel. But I'm here. What am I supposed to do about it?

60

Lou has found a new job.

CUDDLER

You would probably never in a zillion years guess what it is I do all day. So I'd better tell you right off. (she smiles) I'm a cuddler.

I cuddle babies. I cuddle little preemies. Tiny tiny babies who have nobody who can hold them and give them warmth...
and love...

Funny how it began. (a laugh) I ran out of things to do. My house was clean. My closets were done. I live alone. My husband's gone. My children are grown. And I'm retired. (she laughs again) I worked for thirty years. Cashier. And well...you know...I just love babies. Oh, kids are great. And it's kind of fun to watch them grow up...and sometimes not such fun...(pause) But babies...little...babies...what joy. What possibilities!

When friends ask me what I do all day now that I'm alone I tell them I'm a cuddler and they go WHAT? There I was retired and bored out of my skull if the truth be told. Nothing to do is bad for the spirit, I always say.

So this one morning I was reading the paper with my coffee (she laughs) I always read the paper with my coffee. That's one of the nice things I do for myself. So I'm reading the paper...I read the comics first and then the advice stuff...and I see that the hospital is looking for women to be baby cuddlers. Well. I jumped right up and grabbed the phone and I told whoever it was 'Here I am. I'm ready. And what's a cuddler anyhow?'

The nurses tried to show me how to hold the babies. But I told them right off I knew all that. Didn't I have three of my own? Don't my arms remember how to hold a tiny new person?

Of course I was different then, when my babies were born. Oh, yes! Much. Younger. Dumber. (pause)

So now here I am. Older. Smarter. And boy! Am I a good cuddler? The best. That's what the nurses tell me and of course I believe them. (pause)

The babies love me. And I love them right back. (she smiles) Sometimes...Sometimes, you know, they smile right up at me. Honest. They know. I'm sure they know...

Hallie is sitting on a bank of phones. As each rings, she picks it up automatically.

HOLD FOR THE FUTURE

(As she picks up a phone) Psychic hotline… Please hold for the future… (another phone rings, she picks it up) Psychic hotline… Learn the hidden secrets of your past… (another ringing phone) Psychic hotline… (she picks it up) A friend or relative may be trying to reach you… (another phone rings) Psychic hotline…. Please hold for the next available…
(she puts the phone down, turns to the audience)

I get nine bucks an hour. Nine bucks to sit here and what? Solve the world's problems? I talk. I listen. (pause) Sometimes I get it right.

I get a call from this guy. He's thinking…get this…he's thinking he might kill his wife. So what am I supposed to do? Call the cops? What? I think fast and tell him, 'you don't really want to do that.' Why not? He says. Well…I tell him… 'I see a whole lot of trouble ahead for you if you do that.' Oh. He says. That's it. Oh. And he hangs up.

A kid calls me. Wants to know her future. You're supposed to be psychic, she says. So tell me my life. 'All of it?' I stall. The absolute buzz, she says.

She sounds like a good kid so I give her the full treatment. Great future. Fantastic career. Handsome guy. A couple of kids. So how old are you? I ask her. Ten, she says. Ten! I've got to get moving, she tells me. These are my best years.

I'm impressed. Hell, if I thought like that when I was ten, I'd be someplace else right now. Not sitting here taking in a whole lot of garbage and growing the mother of all major headaches working out what to say back. (pause)

I'm not saying I never get a flash. I'm not saying it's a fat bunch of you-know-what. But a psychic message all the time?

63

Each and every phone call? (pause) Dream on. (she pulls out a stack of worn file cards) We don't get into the computer thing. We figure...you know...this is more...personal. (she flips through the cards) A bright future. A warning. Sympathy. That's a tough one. Sometimes they start to cry and I don't know for sure what's getting to them – their life? Or my incredible understanding? (pause) I've sent messages to dogs. Dead dogs. And to grandpa and grandma. It's sad in a way... Crazy and said. They're lonely. So they think about their grandpa. (pause) Or their dog. Then they grab the phone and call me. (a laugh) It's nothing new, all right? It's all in the history books.

'You've got a problem? Go. Ask The Great Oracle what you're supposed to do.'

(Pause) I'm supposed to know the future. Right? But think about it. Just think about it. If I really knew the future, would I be doing this? (pause) Wouldn't I be doing...I don't know...Wouldn't I be doing...something?

(Phones ring. She ignores them.)

Kelli is just exactly where she doesn't want to be.

KELLI AT THE BEACH

HEY! YOU KIDS! CUT THAT OUT! (she waits briefly) KIDS? (then to audience) Quiet. Quiet is not good. Kids? (she calls off again) Kids? (she waits briefly, then to audience) Maybe they're okay...Kids? (she calls, listens for a beat, then to audience) This was all my mom's idea. 'Oh, fab, Kelli! Awesome! July! The beach! Awesome!' (pause) Well maybe. For her. She can sit on the phone as long as she wants and tool around in the car whenever she wants and I'm stuck here. Stuck. (pause) Babysitting.

And the major thing is...(calls off) Kids? (she listens) I told you! CUT THAT OUT! (she waits, listening, then to audience) Okay...okay...(a sigh) That's better. (a beat)

If my boyfriend was here now that would be different. That would be really fine. But...see...his parents...They've got him on this really long trip. Major major trip. Miles and miles. (a broad gesture)

When he told me...hey, don't laugh...I figured out my mother did it. My mother is very very powerful. Like sometimes you know there she is sitting in front of the TV...just sitting...not watching anything...and I right away get this feeling like what's she cooking up?

You'd really be surprised at the things she can come up with. Like this babysitting thing. Oh, hey! Did I forget to tell you? This was not my idea. My mom plotted it out. I hear her. 'Oh, Kelli is simply magical with children!'

Okay...Kids are okay. But let me give it to you straight. This was all a big fat plot to get me away from Teddie. (mocking) I'm young. There are zillions of boys out there... Trust me. I've heard it all. From my mom, okay? (pause)

Look. Maybe it's true for other people. But I...I'm different...For me he is the only one. No question. That's it. (pause)

When my mother was my age she was working really hard so she could get into the college of her choice and meet my father and have me. (pause)

So here I am. At the awesome beach. And there's my guy...up on a mountain someplace...(pause)

I just wish I could figure out a way to get to be eighteen really fast...and then I can run away with Teddie and we can live like happily ever after... Or something.

(A pause, she listens off, then calls) Hey you kids! WHOA! WHATEVER YOU'RE DOING, FORGET IT! JUST FORGET IT! (pause) ALL RIGHT! ALL RIGHT! (pause) I'M GOING TO TELL YOUR MOM!

She hurries onstage talking to the audience as she runs on.

A ROSE BY ANY OTHER...

OKAY! You wanna hear something *totally unbelievable*? My mom wants to CHANGE HER NAME! Did you hear anything so totally unbelievable?

It's Sally, her name. Her name is Sally. Perfectly good name. She's had it all her life. Now she thinks it's boring. Now she wants to be...get this...get this...Serena! And she doesn't even play tennis...Or if she can't do that then...maybe...Suzy. Suzy with a Z!

My mom's best friend...the one she really hangs with...is Phyillis. Phil for short, okay? Now she's thinking of Perri Jo...Or maybe even...are you ready...P.J. This is a woman my mom's age! So now she wants to change her name...the name her mother gave her probably! To P.J.! For peanut butter and jelly maybe? *What can she be thinking?*

There's this other friend, Norma. She's maybe going with Nonie. (pause) You see the problem? What am I supposed t' do here! This is my mom! We're talking about my mom! (pause) I think she's okay...probably...generally speaking she's okay.

But when she gets herself going on one of her big ideas...I don't know...(she shakes her head) I don't want to like...step on her individuality...or something...but, hey! *This is my mom here!* Sally...Suzy...Serena...I hate to see her embarrass herself. And just forget what this is going to do to me with my friends!

How'm I gonna live with this? (pause) So I'm asking...Anybody! Anybody out there! (to audience) Please! Please! What am I gonna do with this? ANYBODY? PLEASE! PLEASE THROW ME A LINE! LIKE...LIKE...HELP!

Isabella is confiding in her new friend.

ISABELLA

I'm sort of thinking of making a change. I'm thinking of going back to school. Education's a wonderful thing.

On the unemployment...there's this special program. You gotta go back to school. Then they dump you off the unemployment. 'Cause you're educated, right?

I used to like school. Third grade. That was my favorite. We had this teacher...Mrs. Fox. She was big on holidays...any kind of holiday...and we had this one song...I really loved that song...(she sings thinly, sadly)

> Bring a torch, Jeannette Isabella
> Bring a torch to the stable come
> He is born the baby Jesus
> Christ is come...and lo...look... (breaking off)

That's all I know. There was this other thing we learned. This might surprise you...I wasn't too great in school...but these two things are the whole that I remember... (looks in his eyes and recites)

> Of all the fishes in the sea
> The one that swims past me
> Is likely quickest to be et
> But if that happens, don't you fret
> That fish is lucky to be et
> And yet I wonder what would be
> If the fish was you
> That swam by me.

(She makes a small quick bow, carefully, like a child)

Mickey solves a craving.

BUTTERSCOTCH SUNDAE

It's the last hour of the last day of the last week of the worst job of my life. I'd given up trying to feel my fingers, my shoulders, my knees and my feet when this cheerful woman hauls herself over to my window, smiles sweetly at me, asks me for a butterscotch sundae with lots of whipped cream and maybe just a little chocolate shot on the top.

I look at her, right at her, and I begin to bawl. Just bawl. Now the boss lands on me with 'What the H is getting into you? That's a cash customer blast it! Don't you know a cash customer when you can see a cash customer? Blast it!'

I can't stop bawling. I make my head go up and down...to show him I know about cash customers...and my hair is all the time flopping in my face...and I am positively disgracing myself in front of the cash customer...and my boss and the entire beach and I could care less! (pause) I mean the summer is over. Way over! And I've worked myself...my total self...into this nothing person AND I DON'T GIVE A SHIT! (pause)

Back in June it sounded so perfect. Outside job, just dishing out ice cream. Smell the air... Walk the beach... Maybe even get in a swim...(pause) Yeah. When? People eat ice cream all day long and half the night. Did you know that? I'll bet you didn't know that. Well guess what? I didn't know it either. I didn't have a clue!

Say you make a boo-boo. Say you dish up strawberry and the customer really wants vanilla. Too bad, baby. Your so-called pay gets docked. Say you're really, really beat and you toss on marshmallow and peanuts instead of whipped cream and cashews...only God can help you there. Trust me. Fun it's not.

69

So now it's September. The summer is over. My feet...my hands...all say enough already! (pause) But there's the cash customer. And there's the boss. I wipe my face on my apron. I look up at the customer...she's standing right in front of me, patiently waiting...I smile at her weakly and I begin to create a monster sundae...a masterpiece of a sundae...with two kinds of nuts and cherries and whipped cream and so much hot butterscotch sauce that it begins to pour slowly ... deliciously... over the edge of the dish.

I wipe it off neatly. I hand it over to the customer. She admires it. I admire it. I admire it so much that I pick up a bowl and fill it with three kinds of ice cream... chocolate... coffee... and strawberry. I pour out fudge sauce and hot butterscotch sauce and then I sprinkle cashews and almonds and just a little chocolate shot on top. I carry it tenderly to an empty table and I sit down...and I eat the whole entire thing...slowly, scraping the dish.

So now the boss says, 'Okay. You just ate up your paycheck.'

I look at him. I sort of smile. And then I totally focus on what's left of my sundae. (pause)

I make a really mean sundae. (pause)

Ask anybody.

KANGAROO

You are not going to believe this, okay?
(pause)

There's this woman... a friend of my mom actually... and here goes the TOTALLY UNBELIEVABLE PART! She went and bought herself a great new computer. And the poor thing... She's like crying to my mom... She's like totally lost with it. Yeah. (pause) I hear this and I'm thinking Sad. Real sad.

So my mom says 'Hey, You've been wanting to find some kind of a job. Like after school. So how's about this? She definitely needs help...'

So all right. I go to see this woman and she says okay so fast I sort of wish I'd maybe asked for like you know...maybe more.

So anyway, I'm like helping her...and she's so grateful it's scary. To be perfectly honest it's PATHETIC! Okay. We start out with the mouse. I figure that's a good way to start and right away...you're not going to believe this!...Right away it's trouble... Okay? SHE DOESN'T LIKE THE MOUSE, okay? Not just the mouse. Any mouse, okay?

She says if it was only something else... Maybe a kangaroo... or something...she...uh ...she'd feel a whole lot better. (pause)

So what am I supposed to do here? I think about it, right? I talk to her like she would be my baby sister or something. I tell her...get this...I tell her let's just pretend this...this thing here...It's not a mouse, okay? It's maybe a kangaroo. Hey. Hurts nobody, right?

And she wants me to tell them not to change a thing! Because she thinks right now she's getting it and any change will totally do her in!

So I ask my mom...She's her friend, right? I say, mom? Your friend...she's kinda...you know...not too swift.

It's a job, my mom says. 'Good experience and all. And you know she's telling all her friends. Lots more work out there,' my mom says.

I think really hard for about a minute. Then I tell her, 'Mom. The money's really good and all. But I've been thinking maybe...you know...maybe I ought to focus more on homework...and like that...'

Turns out this is the absolute right thing to say. Then I quit, but nicely. I tell the woman I'm finished. I'm brain-fried at the moment, I tell her. 'Oh' she says, 'you poor poor thing. They just pile on the work at your school, I bet.' And I tell her, 'Yeah... (pause) Right.'

Vivian addresses her young computer tutor.

KANGAROO II

So... How old are you really? (pause) Yes. It's relevant. It's relevant to me. You're the teacher. I'm the student. (pause) I'd really like to know. (a beat) Twelve. Uh huh. Twelve.

You've been playing with this thing since when? Kindergarten? Before Kindergarten? Before. (a sigh)

So...uh...you know how this little gizmo works? (a pause) And...uh...that one? And that...that...thing? (a pause)

It's not a mouse. So why do they call it a mouse? Just to confuse me? (pause) I'll tell you the truth... A mouse is not something I feel comfortable with. They could have called it something else. Something like...a kitten... Or even a kangaroo?

A kangaroo is good. I could deal with a kangaroo... (pause) All right. I'm faking it, all right? I'm pretending I know how this thing works. I'm pretending I've been using it since kindergarten. Like you. (pause) Excuse me? Not kindergarten? Preschool (a sigh) Okay. Preschool. (another sigh) Oh, boy. (defensive) I know what I'm doing! I'm faking it. Okay? I move this little thing around like this and that makes the little arrow thing do something and then the other thing...the one I found yesterday...comes up and I...OOPS! What's that supposed to be?

You don't know? Come on! I thought you knew everything! (pause) Oh, good. I feel so much better! You don't know everything after all. (pause) I am serious. I am not making fun of you. But look... I get so tired of being stupid! Just once... just once... I'd like to touch this thing (gesture) and have it do what I want it to do. Just once! (pause)

I have to make friends with it? I have to quit fighting it? OH SURE! (pause) OH RIGHT! (pause) How long do you figure this is going to take? Say hours...days...years...? You'll be in college and I'll be sitting here crying at the computer. (pause)

73

You have a little sister? And a baby brother? OH GREAT! GREAT! You'll be in graduate school and I'll be sitting here with your baby brother. (pause) Brian? Okay. Brian.

You're twelve. So we have how long? Four years? Maybe five. Okay. Five. (pause) What are you saying? Newer models? Oh, no! Oh, please! If I ever ever learn how to do this please don't let them change a thing. Not a thing! (pause) I'm begging you! Please... Please... Write a letter to the company... Or send them a what d' y' call it... a mail thing... and you tell them never never change a thing! Or...I don't know...I'll try. I'll try...I'm not stupid...I can do this...I'm a late starter is all...Look. I never went to preschool...

Pat reveals her new status.

THE RENT COLLECTOR

I told the landlord. I told him. I don't wanna take care a' anybody else's money. I told him. I meant it. Makes me nervous.

Like that time I was saving up for a TV and I kept putting away these dollar bills in an envelope and then I couldn't find the G...D...envelope?

So I hadda tell him. I can't collect the rents. Makes me too nervous. 'Just for a few months,' he says. 'Just t' help me out. I'm in a bind here,' he says. 'Who am I gonna ask? The upstairs, they're well...you know...'

I'm not saying a word. But I figure he means that window they broke and the door they kicked in.

'An' the downstairs,' he says. 'They're not home very much.' Home very much! Ha! They put him away – Ten to twenty. And she's all the time running to see him.

So that leaves me. And I'm telling him I can't. I don't wanna take care a' anybody else's money. What if I lose it? I'm the one that has t' pay it back.

'Well look,' he says. 'I'll make it worth your while. I'll knock something off your rent.'

So okay. Here I am. The rent collector. Take a look. That's me. Sort of...

A bare stage. A young woman, busy, with a phone, a pencil, a pad of paper. Sherry, the young woman, is speaking.

MS. NOBODY SPECIAL

(on phone)

Hold on! Hold on! Can you hear me okay? (a pause) Barb? I'm supposed to be doing an interview here. SAY SOMETHING. (a pause) What do you mean 'What?' Say something...you know. Something with a bite. (a wry smile) Something I can quote you on...Something wonderful. (pause)

Sure. Sure. I know. I know you're nobody special. (She laughs) That's the whole idea, Barb. I'm interviewing Ms. Nobody Special. (she laughs again) So talk to me. Tell me your hopes your dreams your... (pause)

No, I'm not paying for this! (rising) What are friends for? (pause) Okay. (a sigh) You'll be famous. Gorgeous hunks you never ever hoped to date in your totally wildest fantasies will be knocking at your door, okay? (a shrug) Maybe even knocking it down. Taking you out to dinner...sending you huge bunches of...what're your favorite flowers? Iris? (a small frown) Okay. Huge bunches of iris that what...? That match your eyes. Ooooh Nice. This is going to be good, Barb. (she sits) You will be SO glad you did this. Hey you're saving my neck. So. Okay. (listening) You love children?

Oh, that's nice. (hopeful) That's good. How about food? How about cooking? How about? (pause)...Restaurants? (a small

76

frown) Well okay. But I was thinking more like...you're a real homebody and you simply love to cook and you and your iris eyes would just adore cooking for some guy... (pause)

Who? Well. The guy who's knocking down your door, that's who. (pause) Look. Barb. Friend. Please. Read me here. I'm stuck. I'm desperate. I'm about to get myself fired! (pause) Well...I...you...know...I...maybe...uh...I maybe...made up a few interviews. (bravely) I know. (pause) I know.

I know I'm not supposed to do that.
Newspapers are supposed to tell you what actually happens. They're supposed to tell you what people really say. I know that. And I did that. I did it for a long time. But I've got to tell you, it can be so damn boring! First you have to dig up somebody to talk to. Then you have to get them to want to talk to you. Then you have to hope they'll find it in their tiny hearts and minds to say something a wee bit interesting...when you know what they could say to make people want to read about it...talk about it...maybe set you up for the best human interest story of the year.

A prize maybe. So maybe you find them. Maybe they talk. Maybe they're boring as Hell! And you've got a deadline. SO WHAT DO YOU DO? (pause) What did I do? (small voice) I...uh...I sort of...helped. Okay? I made it better. I improved on it. They should THANK me for Godssake! They should bless me! They should appreciate the creativity! (pause) Yeah. Well. They didn't, okay? They phoned. They faxed. They did their little e-mail thing. They nearly got me fired. (pause) Yeah. Well. They got me fired. But I'm getting my job back. YOU'RE my ticket back, okay?

So. Let's get moving on this. Iris, okay?

You love iris. And cooking. (pause) No? No cooking? Okay. Restaurants. Listen. Are you sure? There's something about cooking. Cooking would give a kind of an edge. A neat homey feeling, sort of...(a hopeful pause) Apple crisp? (pause) Gingerbread? (pause) Okay. Okay. Restaurants... (she writes) Dick's Diner. Kentucky...what? Uh. Barb. How about movies? Favorite movies? (pause) Or maybe...(hopefully) travel? A trip to...wherever...? Please! Barb! Please! I'm begging! Look. I'll pay you! I know I said that. But I'm desperate here. Come on, Barb. Say something wonderful! Or I'm going to make it up...(she is listening on the phone, hopeful, as lights fade)

Andi has fears and she may be right.

FIREWORKS

My mom says green is the color of jealous. It's a funny. Right? Well maybe it's a funny. Maybe it's not. (pause) See, my eyes are green. But my husband's eyes are greener. From watching me, Mom says.

See, he's really really jealous. Whit is totally nuts! I mean, there is absolutely no reason. I love this guy. Totally. But hey...he won't let me out of his sight.
Except when he's out of town...

He travels a lot. Business. Well all right. Maybe it's business, maybe it's something else. How would I know? I talk to my mom. She says it's really important to keep him interested. (a shrug) Well he's interested. That's not the problem. So then she goes 'Maybe a little jealousy can't hurt.' Well I don't know...There's no way I'm going to fool around to make him jealous. So I figure I'll show him my scrapbook. Old boyfriends...I've got them pasted up in a big book... (pause) Well! Here it comes! Fireworks! He's screaming and yelling and grabbing the scrapbook out of my hand and then he comes after me. Oh yeah. He lands a few good ones. I grab the phone and call the cops. They turn up...finally...and first off they tell me to put my clothes on and then they tell my husband he (mocking) really shouldn't do that anymore. And he says all right. Says he'll never do that anymore.

I call my mom. I tell her I'm scared. 'Walk out,' she says. 'Right now. You want to teach him a lesson.'

'Okay, Mom,' I tell her. 'I'm teaching. I'm walking.' So I go to my mom's place and who comes over with this gigantic bunch of roses...promising everything? So I go back. Yeah, I know.

79

But I go back all the same and it's okay, sort of...But I feel like I'm in jail...or something. He's watching me...I go to the hairdresser...there he is waiting. Aerobics? 'I'll take you,' he says. 'I'll pick you up...' (pause)

I just wish I could really believe he loves me the way he keeps on saying he does. But I have these weird feelings...and I'm scared. I know it's nuts...But I'm telling you the truth. (pause)

I'm really really scared. (pause) Of him.

She enters in a breathless whirl, glances over at the audience with a seductive smile, one arm outstretched over her head. Then, abruptly anxious, she waves her hand and smiles hopefully.

ICON

Hi. (a pause, she smiles again, uncertain) It's me. Honest. I'm here. (she smiles again, hopeful) It's like I never left. (pause) Right?

I went to see my mother the other day. Yesterday. I think it was yesterday. (she shrugs, apologetic) The time thing. I get a little mixed up. Anyway...I went to see her in that place where she is. I went right up to her and said, 'Hi'...and she said, 'Hello?' in that kind of a funny way, like you know how you do when you don't know exactly who you're supposed to be talking to...So I said, 'Ma! Hi! It's me!'

'Oh,' she said. 'Oh, I thought you died.' Well...I mean...I've been gone a while. But I don't think *dead*. I think...you know (a shrug) I think...*resting*. (pause)

When I was young I wanted to make something of myself. I wore tight sweaters and tight little skirts. Actually, one sweater and one skirt. Who had money for more? Guys kept finding me and I kept finding guys. I figured they'd help me. I'd give them what they wanted and they'd help me figure out who I was. And sometimes...sometimes I have to laugh...I'd sit and wonder what those guys would think if they knew who I truly was. 'Course if I know who I was I could tell them. But I didn't, so I couldn't. And they couldn't. Help me, I mean. Not so much anyhow. And they tried...some of them. And I was so scared (a small laugh) Trust me. Truly deeply scared. Oh, Lord!

(she tosses her head, laughing)

Look friends. I'll let you in on a little secret. *I* invented *me*. I made me up. I smiled. (she smiles) I teased. (she poses) I stuck out my front. I stuck out my rear. It worked. So why not?

81

(a shrug) It worked for me like nothing else. Nothing in this crazy world. (pause)

I had this little voice. I thought I needed lessons. Voice lessons. But see...the voice worked out *just fine*. So the voice...the tease...the shape...That's me. I'm it.
(pause, she frowns)

I told you about my mother. She's...not...just right. And it's not her fault. Her mother was the same way. I never knew that. I just found out lately, okay? If I'd figured that out before I think I would've given up completely. So all the time I'm trying to be what everybody thought I was. (she poses) Sexy. Funny. (a laugh) Smart. (she poses again) And all the time I was just me...trying...trying...trying...

So I'm asking you. Everybody. Here I am. Me. The real. I'm here and I need to know. (an anxious smile) I need to know if you believe me. 'Cause it's sort of like that thing, y'know...where whats-her-name...Tinkerbell? Where she says, 'Do you believe?' and they do, so she's there.

So do you believe I'm here? That would be nice. But, hey. Look. Don't worry about me. (she smiles slowly) This is easy. Honest. I don't have to try anymore. I just sort of...well...you know...I just sort of...*am*.

(She waves her fingers in a flirtatious farewell, smiles enticingly over one shoulder)

She enters, elegantly dressed, poised, and confident.

BANDED WITH RIBBON

Never mind what they tell you. I AM TOTALLY INNOCENT! TOTALLY! (pause) Well...all right...Maybe I...maybe...hedged a little...just a tiny bit...(gesture)

Maybe I didn't exactly...precisely...measured by the...(a shrug) the...you know...the yardstick...maybe I fudged...just that much (a small gesture) But...hey! Wouldn't you?

I mean really. Going to...you know...prison. (pause) Going to prison is not one of my top things. I mean really I have so many other things to do. Places to go. People to see.

And time is marching. Marching. Marching. Marching right along. A woman knows this. Time...time...time...it goes. It goes. (pause) I've tried, you know. I've tried. I've tried to stop it. But what can I do all by myself? (gesture)

Maybe...(hopeful) maybe if we all banded together? (a smile) Oh, yes. Banded together! *With ribbon*, I think. Multicolored. Oh, how lovely! How lovely that could be! (small pause)

Grosgrain, I think. With the edges pinked...just a tiny bit... Oh, my yes! (she smiles) And now...where was I?

Oh, my. Who said that? (she smiles) Now who would ask me that? (a glance at the audience)

Stay with ribbon. (a gesture) Stay with pretty. Although...I must say...a stock certificate is attractive...in it's own rather special way. Especially if it...you know...(she smiles) if it stands for...you know...*something*. (she smiles again) Something attractive...something...you know...something rising. Not falling. Falling...you know...is not good...I mean...what does that do for you, after all? WHAT DOES THAT DO FOR YOU? Think of it this way.

Rising is good. Falling is not good.
(a pause, she is not smiling now)

And after all...sixteen months is not so very long. (a shrug) Time for...(sigh) ideas...Time for thinking... Time for...you know...(a tired smile) Time.

Missy has concerns.

HOW I FEEL ABOUT EVERYTHING

I feel awful. I mean really awful. I mean it was not supposed to happen like this. I mean it was you know, for fun.

Who knew I could pull it off? Who knew it would work? It was, look, you know, a joke. Look. I've never been so high-rated on the dating scale. I mean look, I'm okay. But I've never gotten really lucky with guys my age. And I've got to tell you...there aren't enough of them anyhow. I mean available.

So. Older men. Of course a lot of them are married. And that can be a problem. But you now I try not to think about problems. I mean I have enough to think about. My hair. My clothes. My car. My job. It's a whole lot to juggle and I always have to be thinking. What is really first? What is number one? Is it the clothes? The hair? The job? Or is it...him? And you know it's him. It's always him.

But without the clothes and the car and the job where am I? I'll tell you where I am. No place.

So when I got this job I kissed my old boyfriend goodbye and sent him back to his wife so I could concentrate all my energies on this new opportunity. And wouldn't you know. My new boss was just adorable! I tell you I fell. He is just so cute. And married. Yeah. Well...

But we were so careful. I mean we were so discreet. I hardly told a soul. Only my very best friend in all the world and I just knew she'd die before she said a word... So what do you think about a best friend who blabs?

What a mess. What a truly horrific mess. Oh, yeah. His wife knows. And so do a whole lot of other people. And I'm in the like...doghouse. (a shrug) And he is in such deep trouble and I guess it's my fault. Well...sort of...I feel awful about it. Strictly awful. (a pause)

85

And I need to find a new job. Really. And who is going to hire me now? (pause)

I sort of feel like I'm in a movie someplace. Someplace really far away. Maybe China or someplace. I'm sitting there watching this awful movie and Boom! All of a sudden it stops dead and everybody sort of looks around at everybody else, trying to figure out what happened. Nothing. Zip.

Finally somebody comes in and says, 'You're in the wrong movie. If you can wait a little while we'll try and get the right one for you, okay?'

But then everybody gets up and goes and here I am sitting in the dark all by myself waiting to see the rest of this truly terrible movie. And I've got to tell you...I'm pretty sure I don't want to know how it comes out...

Alida reflects on her new life.

ALIDA

When I came here with my boyfriend, I could not believe this place. What a place! What a beautiful place! Look how they live here! Look how they are!

I was so, so happy. I thought I was in Heaven for sure. And then...and then...my boyfriend...he left. (gesture) Like that. He left.

We were living in a room. One room in a house. Like a boarding house you call it. But no food. No kitchen. Nothing. One room. And he left. To go home and see his Papa, he said. His Papa was sick, he said. He would be back in one week. Two weeks. Two weeks the most. (pause)
He would come back for me.

I wait. Alone. One long day. Two long days. Alone. On the third day I walk down the hall. There is a woman in the hall. Young. Like me. She smiles at me and she brings me into her room. A large room with a tiny kitchen. She offers me food. Coffee. Bread. Lucky for me she speaks my language. She listens to me, quiet, nice. She tells me I should maybe think about work. A job. A job? I think. A job? What can I do in this strange place?

Now the landlord is knocking at the door. For money. I have no money. He left so fast, my boyfriend. I never thought of money. What I thought was alone. I am alone. I am alone in this one room in a city I see from my window. A city with the people running so fast this way and that way. I open the window and a rush of cold air surprises me. I pull my sweater around me tight and I wish now I had never thought to leave my home.

Again I see my friend in the hall. I call her friend. She is all the friend I have here.

'You can find a job,' she tells me. 'You can work. They pay good money for people to work.'

87

'What kind of work is this?' I ask.

'You clean for people,' she tells me. 'They pay you to clean the house…'

'In my home we have maids who do this,' I tell her. 'I never do this.'

Again the landlord comes to the door. For money. And I have no money and only the good God knows when my boyfriend will come back for me.

'All right then,' I say to my friend. 'Where is this cleaning please?'

And she tells me. (beat) And she takes me. (beat) And here I am.

Angel on the phone, selling.

ANGEL CALLING FROM WHEREVER

Hey! Yeah! It's Angel! (eager) Yeah. I'm calling about a free vacation. (pause) Yeah. Right! A lousy hundred bucks an' we'll book y' right off f' this terrific free vacation! (pause) Well, hey. That's a freebie...practically. Like where can y' go f' a lousy... (she realizes nobody is on the phone, turning to audience) See! Y'see? THAT'S EVERY TIME! EVERY BLASTED TIME! They hang up on me. No thanks. No goodbye...No have a nice day...Nothing. (pause)

I get started okay. I tell 'em right off it's Angel calling an' I've got this terrific deal. Just for you! A free trip, I tell 'em...And right away I'm like talking t' the air. (pause)

Angel...that's not my real name. We're not supposed t' give out our real names. (a shrug) So, okay, I tell them I'm Angel. (pause) Who could hang up on an Angel?

I swiped my brother's name...Angel. Yeah. He's not exactly...y' know...an Angel. (she laughs) But that's the name my momma gave him. (she laughs)

My brother he...he got himself in a kind of a...situation. (pause) He hadda knife...(pause) Anyhow, he's out of town right now. That's what we tell anybody who comes around looking f' him. Like the cops, okay?

(A beat.) Shel? (calling off) Yeah. (pause) Yeah. (pause) Okay. I'm doin' it, okay? (then to audience) Shel...She's the boss of all of us. She gives me 'C'mon Angel! Sell! GIVE IT THE OLD ONE TWO. (pause)

When she gets really mad she goes YOU BETTER SHAPE UP ANGEL! THEY'LL SHIP YOUR JOB OVER TO INDIA! MAYBE SHIP YOU OVER WITH IT! (a pause) (to audience) So. (a big smile) Where can y' go f' a lousy hundred bucks? We'll book y' right off to maybe win a gorgeous Caribbean vacation? (she waits, hopeful)

Well. Hey. (a shrug) If you're not gonna go f' the great free trip…There's maybe this other thing…(calling off) Hey! Shel! (hopeless) What's that other thing? What's that I'm supposed to maybe tell them if they don't go f' the great free trip? (a pause, she listens off) Whoa! Shel! Not that! NOT INDIA…(pause)
I'm pretty sure my Momma needs me here right now.
(long pause, then to audience) Yeah. Hey, it's a freebie…Practically. You give me a lousy hundred bucks. And I give you this great trip. Okay? (She waits. Silence)
SHEL! HEY! (calling off) NOT INDIA…Okay. Okay. I'll try! (pause, directly to audience) So. You give me a lousy hundred bucks, okay? An' I'm gonna give YOU this GREAT TRIP! Okay? (she waits. Silence. She calls off, helpless) Shel…?! (pleading) Not India, Okay?! Maybe…maybe…someplace else? …Okay...??
(She waits, silence)

When Hedy Lamarr was young, she was internationally famous as a glamorous movie star. In time, she was also the co-inventor of an important scientific invention. Here, many years later, she has been asked to speak about her life.

TRIBUTE TO H.L.

Thank you for inviting me to speak with you today. This is truly an honor. (pause) So to begin . . .(pause)

We are told that modesty is . . .what? A virtue? Yet to be truly honest I must tell the truth. Yes? And the truth, I must say, is that when I was young I was both beautiful . . . and with brains. So. (pause) What is beauty? Something you are given. And brains? They are also a gift. And they are . . . you know . . . a gift with an 'obligation'. An obligation to somehow. . . *use them* (gesture) This, is why I am here with you today. And I must thank you for the opportunity. (pause)

When I was young, I was very beautiful . Yes? Please understand. I myself take no credit for this. This was simply the way I was. My body. My skin. My hair. My eyes. Beautiful. (laughing) I was so lovely I became. . . how do you say. . . a movie star. A star. For my body . Not my mind. My body only. (pause) I was seventeen. (pause)

It was a joke. An amazing joke. They put me in a kind of a (gesture) pool for swimming and in a bathing suit so small with my hair streaming. . . and they tell me 'Swim. . . swim. . . The camera loves you. . . Now swim!' (she laughs)

To me it was a joke. An astonishing kind of a joke. They pay me immense sums of money to photograph my body for anyone to see . . . All over the world like this. (pause) I was not real. Not a person. A thing. An object. A money-making machine. (pause) I was seventeen. Eighteen. Nineteen. Twenty. This was enough. More than enough. I became bored. I wanted to do something with my life. To escape from the nonsense.

91

And there was a man. A rather special man. We fell in love. We married. I told him how I dreamt of freedom . . . Freedom from the . . . the nonsense. And you know he didn't like that? He didn't like that I felt so. He married an icon. And now what did he have? (she smiles, rueful) So. To move on. (pause)

My husband was involved in many projects. When others came to him he liked to show me off. I was to sit and listen. I did this and I heard some astonishing things. Some I could follow. Some not. But everything was wonderfully exciting to me. One day I sat down with a pencil and some paper, and I began to work out an idea for myself.

I struggled with this for a time, rather enjoying the struggle. At the last I went to a friend . . a friend of my husband actually . . . And together we worked it out. (she smiles)

You know the rest of course. (pause) I am here today to accept a great honor, for both of us. Our small invention has brought great change. We created a way for others to follow. We made many things possible that are now . . . every day. (she smiles) And yes, I will say it . . . I am proud. I am extremely proud. This has nothing to do with swimming, swimming in a tiny bathing suit. It has everything to do with me. (a pause, she bows slightly) Thank you. Thank you. (another bow to the audience) I thank you . . .

(Lights fade on her as she continues, gracefully to bow.)

Eleanor Bradley, carefully dressed for hot weather, a light straw hat in her hands, enters from the rear. Smiling, determined, she moves quickly towards a table and several empty chairs downstage, and speaks directly to the unseen occupants.

PORTRAIT WITH PALMS

ELEANOR (cheerful)

Good morning. Good morning. Good morning. You're the young Donelsons, I'm sure. You arrived last night. Am I right? I had every intention of waiting up for you. (gently regretful)

But the plane was so very late. And at my age . . . Oh well. You're here now. Enjoying our lovely morning.
 (sitting)

Well then. Would you like more coffee? I have Rudy in the kitchen. I'm sure he'd be happy to bring you more coffee.
(pause)

Oh, You're cutting down. I see.
(trying)

Such a nuisance about the grapefruit. I'm sure you would have enjoyed some grapefruit with your breakfast. But this dreadful fruit fly thing.
(rising abruptly she calls over the porch railing)

Jock? Are you there Jock?
(pause)
Have you finished the path?
(pause)

93

You'll let me know when you do, will you? (turning away she plants a bright smile on her mouth and once again approaches her guests)

Running a guest house is a busy life.
Forgive me. Now, Tell me . . .
    (brisk, removing her hat, fans face with it)

What are you young people going to do today?
(pause)

Tennis? How lovely! I used to play a lot of tennis when I was a girl . . . On those very same courts. Near the hotel.
(absently)

So many things have changed. But the courts . . . are still the same . . . I'll loan you a racket . . . if you like. (pause)

Nonsense. Take it. I loan it out to guests all the time. (rising she calls, as before)

Jock? (walking again to guest table)

Yes. . . It . . . It . . . was . . . a lovely garden . . .An English garden exactly. But while Jock was away at a school everything slipped away . . (a small silence)

I meant to sell this place, you know. I had a very nice offer. I had quite made up my mind to it. And then. . . I had second thoughts. . . (with regret)

I thought it would be something for Jock. I could retire. He would take over the place. Run it, you know . . . (a pause, she glances out at the garden)

94

And of course all that was long ago. It's close to ... ten years ...
since Jock finished school ... and came back here to live... Jock
loves spear fishing. You must get him to take you spear fishing.
(pause)

Yes, ... it is lovely ... isn't it? (distantly)
Although I'd always planned that when Jock was on his own I'd
give up all this ...
(a gentle wave towards the garden and the unseen sea)
and travel ...

Will you be swimming today? Rudy can pack a light lunch for
you if you wish.. .(rising she calls down to the garden)
Jock? What did they say about the boat? Was that all they said?
(to the table)

Jock had a little accident... With the boat.

Last night.
I've made up my mind. I will not interfere.
Reservations are piled high on his desk.
Unopened. But I will not interfere. (pause)

I would so like to travel ... I'd always planned to travel ...
I want to go to Siam .. And to Hong Kong... To all the places
that I've never been .. I want to go again to England. I want to
go to London. I can live very cheaply in London. I know just
how I'll go. I've had it all planned.
For such a long time. (a pause, then briskly)

I'll fly to New York and from there direct to London. I can pack
everything I'll need in two small bags. I've packed those bags so
often ... in my mind.

I'll go to the North Hotel. I can get a lovely bed-sitting room for twenty guineas a week . . .
And the gardens. . . And the flowers. . . You can go into Harrods and there is a floor as large as from here to over there.
(a broad gesture)

Filled. Simply filled. With masses and masses of cut flowers. Great armfuls of carnations. . . and asters. . . and snapdragon . . and delphinium . . . (pause)

And the country! The English countryside! There's nothing like it here. (gazing out at the view with loathing)

Green fields and hills. . . and no sound of the sea!
I hate the sea! I'm going to get away from the sea! I'm going to turn all this over to Jock . . .
Just as soon as he is ready. I'm going to get away.. . . I'm going to get away from here. . . I'm going to get as far away as I can possibly go! (pause, then quiet, controlled)

So it's tennis this morning, is it? You can take, my racket, if you like. I used to play a lot of tennis . . . when I was a girl . . . (faintly)
On the hotel courts . . . just over there.

A woman enters quietly. She glances at the audience, hesitates, looks down at her hands, then, slowly, begins to speak.

WIFE TO TOLSTOI

I was pouring coffee.
My hand shook.
The coffee ran down the side of the table.
I stared at it... Watching it drip along the
Leg to the rug…Soak in the rug…
I heard words. In his voice.
Words with no meaning.
He wants… To live alone.
Something…
He wants to… Examine his life.
He wants a divorce.
He wants. He wants.

I'm sixty years old. We have three children.

Do I love him? Maybe.
Maybe I hate him.
HOW DO I KNOW?
We've been together thirty seven years.
That's more of my life than I've lived without him…
How do I know if I love him?
HE'S A PART OF ME!

Like a tree.
If you cut off a branch the tree can grow.
What happens if you cut off the TRUNK!

He's not an easy man. My husband.
I'm not easy either.

I rage. I shout. I bolt myself in my room.
And then I rush out and I throw my arms
Around him and I weep when I sense his warm
Strong body next to mine…Puzzled and strange
But next to mine…
For better or worse. Do you take this man? I do.
In sickness or in health…
That was the promise.
The looming shadow was old age…
Sickness…
Death.
Suppose he…
Suppose I…
Suppose we…
Grew sick in our old age.
Like Aunt Lottie. Like Uncle Mel.
Who would take care?
Call the doctor.
Carry the trays.
Hush the dog.
Muffle the doorbell.
Notify the undertaker…
That was the promise.
Not this. Not this…LEAVING
Not this getting rid of EXCESS BAGGAGE!
YOU'VE SERVED YOUR TIME AND I'M DONE WITH YOU
Not this. Oh no. Not this. Not ever.
Not this…

I think about my mother.
My grandmother.
My strong little grandmother.
She married a man she cared for and
Supported until he died.

Until she died.

He never earned a living.
So what? She said. And did it for him
And loved him. Always.

My mother. My mother.
 A beauty. A gentle fortunate beauty.
She married a man who adored her.
Happy ever after. Until her sickness…
She brought me up to be a wife.
I learned the important things.
Duty.
Loyalty.
Faithfulness.
Love.
The wrong things…
I'd like to trade them in.
I'd like to be fierce. Tough. Mean.
I'd like to be mean.
I'd like to fight his way.
I'd like to approach my desk each morning
And carefully plan my victories.
Schedule my triumphs.
Daily weekly monthly.

Call a meeting.
Fire 200 people.
Dump a wife.
Saw off a branch.
Cut down the tree.
I am helpless.
It's a cliché. A tired word. A fact.
He has decided.

His will be done.

He'll be "fair" to me.
I won't "go hungry."
He'll "set up a trust fund."
I'll be "fine."
I won't go begging in the streets...
I won't need. I can't want.
Half of my body will vanish in bloody
Surgery. But I won't need. I can't want.
It's a...promise...
Live on! Live on!
Quit drinking. Run around the block.
You'll live forever. DAMN YOU!
You'll live forever.
Triumphant.
And me? Who knows?
I'll spend my days...How?
Writing spite letters? Shredding his clothes? Ripping old photos?
Closing my mind to the world? Wrapped in comfortable hate like
a warm blanket?
And my nights? How will I spend my nights?
Mourning for the past?
A past that never was?
A past that lived in my mind.
Not in his. In mine. A silly
paradise where we loved each other only.

Forever...and forever...and forever...

Who's to care?
The children? Oh yes. Maybe. For a while.
But they can handle it.

I taught them. I brought them up to be strong.
Hold on. Survive.
I taught them all the things I never knew.
I wanted them to be prepared for life.
Not a Disney world. The real world.
I wanted them to be comfortable in the
real world of danger and opportunity and triumph.

I wanted them to be like him. Not like me.
So they'll be all right. Probably.
Maybe…maybe…he's afraid of growing old.
Maybe he's sick…
Maybe he doesn't understand what he's doing…
To me.
Maybe…

Maybe he's got a brain tumor. It's possible.
When I was a child we had a neighbor who
developed a brain tumor.

He did such very strange things…
Then later…much later…too late to help him…
They discovered a tumor. A tiny wild growth
At the base of the brain. And he died. Leaving his confused and
shrunken family to mourn the stranger that he had become.
Not husband. Not father. Not brother or cousin.
Or son. A stranger.

I loved him once. This stranger.
I love him now.
Love is a habit. A tight habit no swift cruelty can tear.
Trust is a word to forget.
Love is a thing to unlearn.
There is no one. Just myself. No other one.

For the remnant of life that is left to me.
That's it. That's all. Nothing…

Shall I pray for revenge? Stick his image with pins?
Voodoo his miserable pain-ridden death?
Shall I preach on street corners? In parks.
And in malls. 'Don't trust. Don't believe.
Don't…love.'
Shall I chant to a candle? 'Trust believe
Love. Believe love trust. Love trust believe.
I'm fine. He's no good. I'm
Fine. It's not me. It's him. It's HIM!
IT'S HIM!'

I can't accept the gift of this freedom.
So late. His gifts were always…late…
There's a lesson here someplace. If I
Can only find it.
I'm always looking for the lesson.
My children laugh. They say I should have been a teacher.
They're wrong. Not a teacher. A pupil.
Trying to learn. Trying to figure it out.

I know there's an answer. All I have to do
Is find it…

(she stands quiet, alone, as the lights dim.)

A woman at home, alone.

BIRTHDAY

KITTY (on telephone, shouting patiently) IT'S KITTY
MAMMA. CAN YOU HEAR ME? CAN YOU HEAR ME
NOW? (small pause)
I am NOT SHOUTING. I wanted to be sure you could hear me.
DON'T HANG UP! (defeated, she hangs up phone) Damn.
(sighs briefly, pushes her hair off her face, calls again, waits,
then speaks hurriedly)
It's me. It's Kitty. Don't hang up.
(after a small pause)

You hung up on me before, that's why. (brief pause) You
didn't...? Okay...I thought you did.
(eager) Listen, Mamma. Do you know what day this is?
Something special. (pause) No. No...wait a minute. I'm going to
read you something. Don't hang up.

(She hurries to the desk, picks up a colorful folded card, smiles
faintly as she glances at it, then reaches for the telephone)
Now listen... (reads slowly)

'With curly hair
And eyes of blue
Little girl,
I love you.

When you grow up
I know you'll be
As sweet and good
And dear to me.
Happy Birthday.'

(brief pause)
Yes. It is sweet. I loved it…when I was ten.
(small pause, then with slight irritation)
I read it so you'd know what day it was!
(a pause, she waits, expectant, then sadly)

It's my birthday. Not your birthday…
My birthday. Oh God! Can't you remember anything?
(pleading)
Say Happy Birthday. Happy Birthday, Kitty…
Say it mamma…Please!

(after a pause, patiently)
I know you're miserable. I didn't want to put you there. You've got to believe me. It was Lenny. Lenny loves you, Mamma. He was worried about you all the time. He went to work and couldn't think… He couldn't do his work. Worrying about you… Maybe turning on the stove… and forgetting all about it… or wandering around in the street… without a coat… maybe getting hit by a car… Lenny worried a lot about you… He… he really loves you, mamma. In his way…
Well yes…It's true. You could have stayed here with us…
Oh the Hell with it…He didn't want you!
HE DIDN'T WANT YOU IN HIS HOUSE! Old…and
sick…and smelly…
Lenny hates old people. He hates the idea of being old. He hates knowing that he's growing old…
(an attempt at cheerfulness)
Listen, I'm going to have a little drink.
Just a tiny little drink…to celebrate my birthday…I'm going to pretend you're here with me…And we're going to drink to my birthday.

104

(she puts the phone down carefully, hurries to the chest and pours herself a stiff drink from an open bottle of whisky. She takes a good swallow, then another...)

(raising her glass)
To you, Leonard, we give our little girl, Katherine Mae. Now you take care of her. FOR LIFE! That was the promise... And nobody ever broke a promise. Unless...maybe...I did something awful...like run away with the milkman. Then Lenny could...Lenny could...divorce me...
And it would be my fault...and I would suffer. But that would be all right...because it was my fault.
(unsteadily)
It was a package deal. He's welching on the deal, Mamma!
(sadly)
I'm here...and he's here...but he's not gonna be taking care of me anymore...He's gonna be taking care of somebody else...
(dimly, singing)
Some...body...else...is...taking...my
Place...Somebody...else...
(pause)
Singing. I'm singing.
(thoughtfully examining her glass)
I don't know what there is to sing about...
(drinking)
I wasn't going to have this birthday. I was...going...to disappear...I was going to take...a lot of pills...and he'd come home and find me all dead and cold and he'd be sorry and he'd know how much he loved me after all...

(small pause)
I am not boozed up!
(looks at nearly empty glass)
Well...maybe...just a tiny bit...

105

(pause)
Don't call me that. It's an ugly name.
I always hated being Katherine Mae.

(after a short pause, musing)
Papa named me? You never told me that. Why didn't you tell me that?
Why didn't we ever talk about...anything that mattered?
(drinks, emptying the glass)
We talked about...clothes...and boys...and boys...and clothes...and parties...and school...and piano lessons...and thank you notes...and boys...
Why didn't we talk bout you? Or your sister who died when she was young? Or your brother who ran away on his eighteenth birthday? (small pause)
Don't cry, Mamma. Please don't cry.
I didn't want to hurt you. I'm looking for help!
(coaxing)
If you'll be quiet I'll tell you
Something nice...
(with an effort)
I made a lovely dinner last week. I think it was last week...I made your pot roast...and your lemon pudding...and your apple cake. Everybody said it was delicious. Everybody thinks I'm a fabulous cook...But it's not me...
(studying her empty glass)
It's you...
(rises)
Listen...Hang on a minute, okay? I'll...be right back.
(She reaches an arm for the bottle.)
I wish you could remember my birthday...
It's like I was never born when my mother can't remember my birthday...(drink) It's a big one, too.
(small pause)

Not thirty seven, Mamma. Forty seven.
I am forty seven years old. Today.
(waves glass in mid-air)
I want to make a toast! TO ME! To Katherine Ludlow Wallace on her forty-seventh birthday!
(singling idly)
Happy Birthday to me...I'll swim in the sea...I'll jump out a window...Happy Birthday...to...me...
(small pause)
OF COURSE IT'S CHILDISH! I'm still a child, Mamma. Your forty seven year old baby! I've lived on this earth for forty seven years and I don't know a thing! NOT A GOD DAMNED BLASTED LOUSY ROTTEN THING!
(stares at her glass reflectively, then drinks until it's empty)

(Kitty puts down the telephone and walks to the low chest, empty glass in hand. She reaches for the bottle, but sees next to it a small china ornament. She picks it up and it slips from her hand to the floor and breaks. Abruptly she begins to cry. Sobbing, she rushes back to the telephone.)

The bird broke! I broke it...The pretty china bird you gave me...I dropped it...and it broke...It's all in pieces...Little painted pieces...(small pause)
I'm crying because the bird broke...and it's my birthday...
(quiet)
I'm crying...because...I can weep over that silly bird and I can't even tell you why I called! I can't tell you...
What's happening to me...
(no longer crying, she wipes her face, absently, then quietly...)
He's leaving me. Lenny's leaving me.
(louder)
CAN YOU HEAR? LENNY'S LEAVING.
(a small pause, then laughing, bitter)

107

Better to stay with my husband? Better to stay with Lenny? HE'S LEAVING ME, MAMMA. HE'S LEAVING ME! HE DOESN'T WANT ME ANYMORE!
(pause)
What a rotten thing to say. What a lousy rotten thing to say. No, I wouldn't rather he was dead!
But then he wouldn't have a choice...
Wouldn't he? And he's NOT DEAD! He's alive...and he wants somebody else...NOT ME! HE WANTS THAT SLUT...that...that...GOD DAMNED PIECE OF SHIT! THAT THIRTY YEAR OLD...STREETWALKER!

(a pause, then dully)
What children? Mamma, I've only got one...Remember? Deedee's grown up. She doesn't need me. She has her own life... Ever since he told me...I...I can't seem to do anything...I...go through the motions...But I can't do anything...
(rubs her fingers nervously)
I can't think...I can't decide...the simplest things...
Like what to eat for breakfast.

And I dream. The strangest dreams. Last night I dreamt of a ladder...all made of flowers...it went into the sky. I tried to climb it...And it broke...And I fell...and I fell...I really ought to leave him...It would be better for me...
If I could be the one to leave...

(she wanders, distractedly, to the closet, pulls out a suitcase, opens it, then opens a bureau drawer absently, picks up a few assorted pieces of clothing, uncaringly tosses them into the open suitcase. She starts to cry quietly, head in hands. After a minute, she glances up, wipes her face half-heartedly, and tries to compose herself. She sees the phone off the hook, replaces it slowly, vaguely walks back to the bureau, finds something, a scarf perhaps, holds it to her mirror image briefly, tosses it into the suitcase. The telephone rings. She hurries to pick it up)

(on telephone, hastily, feverishly)
I'm leaving mamma. I'm leaving him...
I'm leaving him before he gets a chance to leave me...I...
(abrupt change of tone)
You're what? You're who? WHO IS THIS?
What? Look...I don't want any photographs...
Please...I don't care if they're free...
(building, frantic)
No really...Look...If you'll hang up now we'll all come down tomorrow...You can take all the pictures you want...tomorrow! If you'll just hang up...PLEASE HANG UP! OH MY GOD HANG UP!
(she hangs up the telephone, then calls frantically)

Mamma! Mamma! Are you there?
(small pause)
I did not hang up on you! You hung up on me. Yes you did. I swear you did...(weeping softly)
Why did you do that? That wasn't very nice of you.
(a pause, then quietly)
Lenny's father died. Did I tell you?
(wiping her eyes)
He carried on like a baby...
(pause)
He's not throwing me out. I can stay here. He says I can stay here...But I don't think I should. I'm going to leave...Just as soon as I...
(weakly)
get packed...and everything...
(plucking at her shirt, then abruptly)
Personal question. Very personal question.

109

(bravely)

Why did you stay with Papa? Why didn't you leave him? Ever think of leaving him?

(brief pause)

I saw him hit you...

(low)

I SAID I SAW HIM HIT YOU. You didn't know...But I saw...I was ashamed for him. I was ashamed for you, too. Why did you...just stand there? Why didn't you walk out? Why did you...take a suitcase...and walk out?

(a pause, then careful, incredulous)

You stayed because of me. You knew I wouldn't ask you. You stayed because I needed a father.

OH THAT'S FUNNY! THAT'S VERY FUNNY!

WHAT KIND OF A FATHER WAS HE?

LOUSY! LOUSY! LOUSY!

He wasn't a father. He was the man who went to work and came home.

I was so afraid of him. I twisted myself inside out to please him...to be sweet...to be good...

(low)

I thought he'd love me...more...if I was good...And I was afraid! I was terrified! Every time he screamed at you I was sick to my stomach. Did you know that, mamma?

EVERY GOD DAMNED TIME.

(quietly)

I used to pray that maybe one morning he'd wake up feeling good. He'd pat me on the head and call me Kitten...and he wouldn't holler at breakfast...and I could go to school without throwing up...

And you stayed with him for me?

(drinks)

110

WHAT A LIE! WHAT A GODDAMNED LIE! DON'T GIVE ME THAT BULLSHIT!
(sobbing)
You were afraid…Where would you go? What would you do? YOU COULDN'T LEAVE HIM COULD YOU? YOU WANTED TO OH HOW YOU WANTED TO BUT YOU DIDN'T DARE, DID YOU?
(quiet, low)
You didn't dare…I'm ashamed…because you didn't dare…Silly…It was so long ago…What does it matter now?

Who taught you that marriage was some kind of magic? And you taught me and I taught Deedee…
(mocking)
Magic. Marriage…marriage…magic…
(sings, waving her glass)
Here comes the Bride…all dressed in white…
White dress…white shoes…white veil…All white. For purity…for goodness…and forever…
I lied to you…before…about the pills…
(low)
I…I did it…I tried…but it didn't work…I guess I didn't take enough…I just got sleepy…I got so sleepy…
(toneless)
Somebody…found me…and then they made me walk around…and around…and around…They wouldn't let me sleep…and I was so sleepy…
(small pause, then dully)
I promise…I'll never try it again…I promise.

(abruptly she stands, slightly uncertain of her balance)

I'm gonna think about my birthday….

(tries to touch her toes, and fails)
I'm gonna concentrate on my birthday.
(smiling)
I'm gonna make a party. Nobody else gonna make it...I'm gonna make it...
(shouting happily into phone)
You wanna come to my party?
(then ignoring phone)
I'm gonna have cake...and...surprises...lots of stuff...

(scrambles on her hands and knees looking for something under the bed. During the following speech she finds it, a large white box tied with a ribbon, hauls it out happily, and opens it)
Bought myself a birthday present...Nobody else...gonna give me a present...Gonna have a nice surprise present...gonna look great for my birthday...

(suddenly she abandons the box and runs to the phone)

Mamma...I'm gonna look nice for my birthday!
(small pause)
I thought you'd like that.
I'll look nice...and pretty...
(small pause)
Everybody always said I was pretty...
(anxious)
I was a pretty girl, wasn't I?
(low, to herself)
Everybody said...I was a pretty girl...

(abandoning the telephone, she runs to the mirror and desperately examines her tear-stained face. She pushes her hair back, off her face, and stares into the mirror, then hurries to her birthday box. She opens it, fingers shaking, and pulls out a bright red tunic and

112

soft black pants. She holds the tunic to her body, tentatively, not looking in the mirror, and murmurs...)

I'm going to wear my new red tunic...and my black silk pants...and my red sandals...and my dangly earrings...that Lenny gave me...last year...
(she leaves the tunic and pants and runs, distracted, to the window...calling...)
I'm going to have a party...Will you come to my party...
(dashes wildly to the closet, comes back with a single red sandal clutched in one hand)
(calling wildly, distractedly)
We'll have caviar! And champagne!
And music! And flowers! And people...Lots and lots of people! Everybody.

ALL MY FRIENDS!
(build)
I want to hear people laughing...
I'll wear my red tunic...and my shiny black pants...and I'll laugh...with my friends...and they'll drink a toast...to my birthday...And they'll wish me many...many...more...Many...more...

(she runs eagerly to the telephone, off the hook, picks it up and calls happily)

It's my birthday, Mamma!
I'm going to have a party...
Will you come to my party...
I'm going to wear...my red...satin top...and my black pants...and we're having champagne...and caviar...and music...
(frantic)

Is everything ready...?! I've got...to get...everything...

(She runs to the closet, pulls out armfuls of clothes, anything, dumps them in the open suitcase. Then she runs to the bureau, pulls out an entire drawer, empties everything in a mass on the floor. She sees the red tunic, forgotten on the bed, picks it up feverishly, struggles with it, pulls at the buttons, tries to pull it over her head, gives up, defeated. She picks up the red sandal and feebly heaves it at the wall. She puts her head in her hands and sobs wildly)

Don't leave me...Don't leave me...
Please don't leave me....What am I going to do?
WHAT AM I GOING TO DO!
Don't leave me Mamma...Don't leave me Lenny...
Please! Please! Don't...leave...

An old woman sits alone. A telephone and a small flowering plant are on a table next to her chair. A TV set is in a corner of the room.

WHOSE BIRTHDAY?

WOMAN

(her hand is on the phone, she has just replaced the receiver)

Why does she talk so much...that woman?
Maybe she's lonely. I suppose she's lonely...
I remember being lonely. Days. And nights.
Sometimes I'd weep. For loneliness.
Maybe she's like that. So she calls me.
(smiling)

What do you think? You...sitting there?
What do you think, 'eh?

(she picks a leaf off the geranium plant, crumples it in her fingers, sniffs delightedly, abandons it)

Nothing. You say nothing. Well you're not meant to talk, 'eh?
If God meant you to talk, he'd give you a mouth.

(abruptly she closes her eyes, dozes briefly. The telephone rings, incessant, near her hand. She ignores it. The ringing continues. Unwilling, she picks up the receiver at last, holds it to her ear for a short moment, then saying nothing, she hangs up.)

It's her. Let her cry. I don't want to hear.

(the telephone rings again. She sits patiently, not answering, waiting for the ringing to stop)

I want to think. I have a lot…to think about…
My father. My mother. My sisters…
My brother…
And him. I think about him too…
Sometimes…
So long ago. It's so long ago…
They tie me in the chair. So I won't fall out. Maybe break something. My head maybe…
(smiling at her feeble joke)

What difference? What difference?
If I fall. If I break myself in pieces. Little…tiny…pieces…
Like a cracked tea cup. Who's to care?
I've grown so small. Like a bird.
A withered bird.

(laughing)

An antique. That's what I am. An antique.

(laughing)

You manage…somehow…God knows how…
To live a long time…And then…all of a sudden…
You're an antique!

(The telephone rings. She ignores it deliberately, talking over the insistent sound.)

For God's sake! Shut up you...You THING...You!
(the ringing stops)

If I want to talk on the telephone I'll talk on the telephone. And if I don't...I won't. And THAT'S IT.

(There is a small silence. The telephone rings again. She looks at it, wondering, but makes no attempt to answer)

Her. I'll bet it's her. Who else calls me?

(The ringing stops)

Poor thing. Poor kleinshike. I'm sorry for her. I pity her...in my heart...

(The telephone is silent. She picks it up, listens intently, replaces the receiver, says nothing, touches it absently)

She calls me mamma. Why? It's some kind of a trick? She's not my mamma. My mamma died a long time ago. A long time ago...I don't know exactly how long...
(a small silence)

I had a daughter once...once...Such a pretty girl. With long curls...Such beautiful curls...How I used to love to brush those curls. Make a bow with the ribbon and tie the curls back from her sweet face...
(sigh)

117

I had a daughter. A long time ago.
I had a daughter. I had a husband...
(a silence)

He came from Russia. Not exactly Russia. Near the border. I don't remember exactly. It's so hard to remember... He was handsome. So handsome. And strong. Like an ox he was so strong...

I admired that.
Later...I...Later many times I could wish he was
Less strong...I don't want to think about that.

Why did I marry him? Who knows?
For spite maybe. To show everybody.
I don't know... If I could remember why I married him
(she laughs abruptly)

Maybe when I see him...I'll ask him. I'll walk right up to him...and I'll ask him. Loud. In front of everybody. Like he would do.

'Tell me...' I'll say. 'Tell me something...'
'Sure' he says.
'Tell me...' I challenge him...looking up at his great height...his heavy arms...his red beard... 'Tell me why I married you...'
He begins to sputter and to choke. He is angry. So angry. The temper rising. And he can't answer me. How can he? He doesn't know. I don't know. I never understood myself.
Why I married him...

(The telephone rings. She stares at it absently, making no move to pick it up. After a moment the ringing stops. She stares at the now silent phone pensively)

This one. She had a hard life. Rich... I think... But a hard life all the same. The husband doesn't love her, she says.
Ah, 'love.' What is 'love?' Did he ever 'love' her?
But to her I say nothing. I listen.
She's lonely. There's nobody to talk to...
I know that feeling. So I listen.
(a silence)

A crazy old lady with hair falling over her face...
She came to the door...crying...
I was stronger then.
I ran fast. So fast.
I ran home. To my house. My darling little house.
When I got there a stranger was there.
Living in my house.
He called the police. And they came.
And I cried.
They brought me back here. So here I am. And here I'll stay.
Until I die... (a silence)

I suppose...it's not so bad. It could be worse. They're nice to me...
NICE! What am I saying! NICE!
They're little devils! Is a devil NICE?
They lie...
'You're getting better...You'll be fine...Soon you'll go home...'

I am never going home. They know it.
I know it...

119

And they steal. Whatever they can take.
They take it. So it's not exactly stealing.
They take. (musing) The funny thing. They take. To torment me.
Then they put it back. Did you ever hear of such a crazy thing?
Meshuganah. Take and put back.

(she turns restlessly in the chair.)

I'm tired of sitting in this chair. (petulant) Why doesn't somebody come to let me out…?
Once…A long time ago… (confiding)
Once I got out. I ran away. Yes I did. I did. I couldn't do it now…

VOICE (on television, weary)

If you're going to tell me that I'm the only one who means anything to you, Simon, I think I'll vomit.
(telephone rings on television)
Amanda darling! Simon was just telling me about your…what should I call it…
Your…date? Of course I will…When I see him…

(loudly) Back off, Simon! If you raise one hand against me…I'll…I'll…call the POLICE!
(she snaps off the television absently)

The police. The police brought me back.
I could hardly blame them. In my heart. They were afraid…I suppose…

(a small laugh)
Maybe they thought…Maybe they thought I'd die…on the spot.
Right there. And then what could they do? What could they say?

Maybe they thought...Maybe they thought I'd die...on the spot.
Right there. And then what could they do? What could they say?

(the telephone rings. She lifts her head to stare at it, distantly.
The ringing ceases. She stares at her hand absently)

When I came here first...I had a ring...
A little ring. With a stone. Such a pretty stone. Blue.
I loved that little ring. And now...
It's gone...
When I ask where is the ring...They
Tell me in the safe. Why should I believe them? Why the safe?
So many years I had it on my finger. So now they put it in the
safe...where I can't have it...and I can't see it...
What good is that...?
I used to have to hold it to the light...
And look at it...and think.
He gave it to me when she was born.
Kitty. My kleinshike Kitty. And now
She's gone...Like him. Like everybody
She's gone.

(the telephone rings. She turns in her chair promptly, picks it up,
shouting fiercely into the phone)

LEAVE ME ALONE!
 WHY DON'T YOU LEAVE ME ALONE!
Talk to somebody else about your troubles!

(without waiting for a reply, she hangs up angrily. The telephone
rings. She picks it up)
Yes? Who are you?
I don't want to talk.
Goodbye.

I don't want to talk. I want to think.
I don't want to hear about your life.
I want to hear about...my...life...
(dimly)
I had a lamb when I was small. A little white lamb. I tied a ribbon and a bell around his neck...and he was so clean.
But then he grew big and my father took him to the slaughter house and butchered him...I could never eat my little lamb...

(a silence, she picks absently at the geranium plant, pulling off leaves without noticing)

Later came the bad time. The people hiding
Inside their houses. Nobody dared to go in the streets. All the windows we kept tight closed...
(a silence, she nods in sudden sleep, then shakes herself awake)
We came here...to this strange place...with fear. Not courage. Fear. Who knew what we might find in here? Could we live? Would there be work? Would there be food...? Who knew? Mamma said yes. But did she know? We cried ourselves to sleep...many nights...on that boat...Jacob and Sara...and Rachel...and me...
(a small silence)

My little lammele. With the pretty ribbon on his neck. Papa bought him to butcher for meat. And we made him a pet. Papa was angry. How can you butcher a pet?

I sang to my little lamb. Like mamma sang to me...before Papa came and carried him off.
Poor Papa. He's been gone a long time. Such a long time. Sometimes I think I see him...

(a sharp whisper)
Sometimes...I'll tell you. Sometimes...I don't WANT to see him. Not now. Someday maybe. Not now.
When Papa comes he'll want to take me with him. I'm not ready for that. Not yet. Not now. Someday...maybe...

(softly she murmurs, half humming, half singing)
Schluff mine feigele...Close the eigele...Lulee Lulee lulee loo...Schluffen mine kind. Schluffe's
(suddenly she starts, terrified)
PAPA! Papa! Is that you, Papa?

(quietly, frantically, she glances around the room from her chair, seeking shadows under the table, by the bed, everywhere)
Papa...Please...PAPA! WHERE ARE YOU? Papa...
Where are you hiding...come...come...come here...
Please...Where can I see you...Papa...

(struggling desperately for control)
Where is mamma...

(glancing)
And Jacob...And Sara...And Rachel...

(softly)
Why...? Why are you here...All of you...?
Why...? It's not time...yet...I don't think it's time...yet...I'm not ready...yet...Papa...I don't think it's time...You go back...Go back...
(widely gesturing)
Go back...I'll let you know...when I want you...I'll find a way...to let you know...
Papa...

123

(telephone rings. She grabs it frantically)
Yes. Hello. Yes. Help me! Can you help me?
They're here. Mamma…and Papa…and Jacob…and Sara…and
little Rachel…They're all here. They've come to take me…
Yes…All right…I won't look…I'll make believe they're not
here…I'll…All right…I'm afraid…

(a silence. She hangs up the telephone slowly, turning in her
chair to shut out her fearful images. After a moment she calls
softly.)

Papa…? Gone? Are you gone?

(telephone rings. She picks it up promptly, listens intently)

There's nobody here. Who told you my Papa was here? He's
gone…They're all…gone…

(she hangs up. Holding telephone in her lap
she gazes at it, unseeing)

Where's my girl?
Why doesn't she think of me?
Why doesn't she come to see me?
Maybe she's…dead.
There's nobody. Only me. And my thoughts.
They drive me wild sometimes…
My thoughts.
If she was alive she'd come to see me
And call me…at least…

(telephone rings. She picks up receiver, listens with careful
concentration, then talks, telephone in lap, to herself)

I hear you lady. I hear you.
Sure. Sure. It's terrible. But it's over.
Done. You'll survive. You get to my age.
You look back and you say to yourself...
There was good. There was bad. But all in all...
I survived.

(loudly, into the telephone)
That's what I wish for you lady...survive.

(she starts to hang up the phone, changes her mind, calls into it)

Lady...you know my girl?
Could you tell her to come and see me?
Call me...maybe
(pause, she listens)

Don't cry lady. There's enough tears
In the world...
Don't make more.

(she sits quietly, phone in her lap, receiver off the hook, waiting)

WOMAN WITH BOOK

There's a picture hanging on the wall of the museum downtown. Second floor turn left at the elevator. A painting of a woman holding a book. She's dressed in purple, my special color. And she's wearing my face. I smile at her and I think that's *me*.

That's me with a book in my hand. That's me with a quirky smile on my mouth. That's me looking out at the world.

Her portrait was painted in seventeen hundred and something. Three hundred years ago.

I stand in front of her and I talk to her in my head. 'I have your face,' I tell her. 'Three hundred years and I have your face.'

'You're gone,' I tell her. 'You're gone and your world is gone. I'm here now,' I tell her. 'And I have your face.'

Appendix

These monologs have been excerpted from the following plays by Jolene Goldenthal:

I'm Going to Marry Wally	BUDDIES
Lottie	THE RETRO BUS
Custard	REMEMBERING RACHEL
Isabella	HOW TO EAT A PIZZA
Portrait with Palms	ISLAND

Jolene Goldenthal is an award-winning playwright whose work has been seen at Hartford Stage, Ensemble Studio, Victory Gardens, Bailiwick Rep, Mill Mountain and Florida Studio Theatre, Mercyhurst College and the 92 nd St Y among others.

She has taught dramatic literature and theater history and is the Founding Artistic Director of The Hartford Playwrights Inc.

Jolene Goldenthal is a former columnist and Art Critic for The Hartford Courant. She is a member of The Dramatists' Guild.

Thanks to the Editors of these publications who first published: A FLOWER OR SOMETHING, in *Best Women's Stage Monologues*, (Smith and Kraus) A FLOWER OR SOMETHING in *Millennium Monologues,* (Meriwether) THE ONE, in *Best Women's Stage Monologues*, (Smith and Kraus) a segment of BIRTHDAY in *Monologues For Women By Women* (Heinemann), and WIFE TO TOLSTOI in *Mequasset By The Sea & Other Plays* (Andrew Mt. Press).